shibui leaf tea

FOR BREW FREAKS, BEAN GEEKS AND THE SIMPLY CURIOUS ...

Calling all
COFFEE
LOVERS

...show your milk the  you show your beans!

Find out more at yeovalley.co.uk

Yeo Valley Organic Whole Milk

Yeo Valley FAMILY FARM

Buy British milk to reduce the food miles in your cup

Our cows are fed on an organic diet, free from pesticides and GMOs

Our farmers are guaranteed a fair price for their milk

So you can rest assured you're getting great taste the right way!

www.saltmedia.co.uk
Tel: 01271 859299
Email: ideas@saltmedia.co.uk

Salt Media *Independent Coffee Guide* team:
Nick Cooper, Sophie Ellis, Clare Hunt, Kathryn Lewis,
Abi Manning, Tamsin Powell, Jo Rees, Rosanna Rothery,
Christopher Sheppard, Dale Stiling, Mark Tibbles and
Selena Young.
Design and illustration: Salt Media

A big thank you to the *Independent Coffee Guide*
committee (meet them on page 190) for their expertise
and enthusiasm, **our headline sponsors** Cimbali,
iZettle, KeepCup, Olam Speciality Coffee and Yeo Valley,
and sponsors Almond Breeze, Arla Foods, Cakesmiths,
Extract Coffee Roasters, Roastworks Coffee Co. and
Shibui Tea.

Coffee shops, cafes and roasters are invited to be
included in the guide based on meeting criteria set by
the committee, which includes the use of speciality
beans, providing a high quality coffee experience for
visitors and being independently run.

For information on the Ireland, The North and North
Wales, and Scottish *Independent Coffee Guides*, visit:

www.indycoffee.guide
🐦 @indycoffeeguide
📷 @indycoffeeguide

HOUSE ESPRESSO
BLACK GOLD Nº3

BLEND OF

BRAZIL - YELLOW BOURBON PULPED NATURAL

COLOMBIA - CATURRA FULLY WASHED

EL SALVADOR - BOURBON FULLY WASHED

NOTES OF RICH CHOCOLATE
AND BISCUIT

SINGLE ORIGI
ESPRESSO

BURUNDI-MPAN
FULLY WASHE

ORANGE ACIDIT
BLACK CHERRY
PEACH WITH A M
CHOCOLATE FIN

COALTOWN

COFFEE

ALL OUR COFFEE IS HAND ROASTED IN
#BRINGBACKBLACKGOLD

COFFEES		SLOW DRIP
ESPRESSO ½o	1.5/2.2	POUROVER
CAPPUCCINO 8/12oz	2.4/2.6	TAKES 4 MINS
FILTER	2.2	SEE BOARD FOR
LATTE	2.4	TODAYS COFFEE
LONG BLACK	2.2	3.0
MACCHIATO	2.2	
MOCHA	2.8	TEAS
PICCOLO	2.3	SELECTION OF TEADROP TEAS
PICCOLO LATTE	2.4	PACKED AT ORIGIN TO
FLAT WHITE	2.5	PRESERVE FRESHNESS

ENGLISH BREAKFAST
PEPPERMINT
EARL GREY   2.2
SPRING GREEN

CHOCOLATE
3.0

Join the #Reuse Revolution & get 25p off T/A drinks

Nº4
COALTOWN ESPRESSO BAR

AKFAST

OAF SOURDOUGH
VALLEY BUTTER
JAM or DARK ROAST NUT BUTTER

N SCRAMBLED EGGS
GH TOAST 6.50

SCRAMBLED EGGS WITH
ASUNDI + SOURDOUGH TOAST 7.00

D LOAF, SMOKED STREAKY
OMATOES + KASUNDI 6.50

SMOKED BACON SARNIE,
ARRED LETTUCE 6.00
(* OR SMOKED TOFU)

TS + ROASTED FRUITS WITH
ASTED ALMONDS + COCONUT FLAKES 4.50

N RAISIN GRANOLA WITH
O YOGHURT 5.00

DRINKS

FRESH ORANGE or
GRAPEFRUIT JUICE 3
MELONADE 2.90
MANGO LASSI 3.00
MANGO ICED TEA 2.55
FRESH FRUIT SMOOTHIE 3
LIME + SODA 2.25
LEMONADE 2.25
ICE CREAM SHAKES:
CHOCOLATE OR
BANANA 3
AFFOGATO 4
COFFEE ON ICE 2.70
PINEAPPLE SODA 2.90
ROOIBOS + ORANGE
ICED TEA 2.90
BREAKFAST
SMOOTHIE 3.50

LUNCH

FED BOWL
- ALL THE SALAD
- ALL THE SALADS WITH
FRITTATA / SAMOSA / SAUSAG

* SOURDOUGH TOASTIES:
- BAY BRAISED RED ONION, S
MATURE CHEDDAR 6.00
- GOATS CHEESE, ROASTED PE
CARAMELIZED ONION 6.50
- BACON JAM, ROCKET +
MATURE CHEDDAR
- BOMBAY ROASTED CHIC
PEANUT CURRY BUTTE
(* ALL OUR TOASTIES ARE SERVE
(PINK PICKLES, GUINDILLAS + BABY

Nº 26
FED 303

CONTENTS

PAGE

I t's hard to believe it's been five years since the coffee-mad team at Salt Media started working on the first *South West Independent Coffee Guide*.

What started as a chance conversation with a couple of industry pioneers (and a hunch that the speciality industry was on the cusp of something special) has grown organically into a collection of independent guide books and a whole lotta caffeinated adventures across the country.

It's fitting that the guides for the indie coffee scene are crafted by an indie publisher, and it's been great to meet so many enthusiastic and like-minded folk at the cafes and roasteries on the journey.

The speciality community in the South West (and in South Wales, which joined the *Indy Coffee Guide* family in 2016) has grown enormously in five years. While not long ago finding a quality flat white in rural Cornwall was harder than a three-point-turn in a country lane, within this fifth edition you'll find 30 new cafes and roasteries across the region to add to your hit list.

The speciality movement continues to build momentum and offer a high quality alternative to the global cafe chains (read all about it in *Right Here, Right Now* on page 16). However, the same passion for the craft and focus on community which ignited the speciality spark in 2014 continues to fuel the coffee fire.

Here's to another year of fantastic coffee.

Kathryn Lewis

Editor

Indy Coffee Guides

🐦 @indycoffeeguide
📷 @indycoffeeguide

HOLD ON TIGHT

THIS IS THE REUSE REVO– LUTION

THE ORIGINAL
BARISTA STANDARD
REUSABLE COFFEE CUP

DESIGN YOURS AT
KEEPCUP.COM

Change has been the only constant in the coffee sphere since the *Indy Coffee Guides* were launched half a decade ago – and developments continue at breakneck speed. We asked some of the South West's speciality insiders about the hot topics charging the scene right now – and where things are heading ...

REBEL ALLIANCE

The indie cafe movement has long been a disrupter to the occupation of our high streets by the big coffee chains. Independently owned speciality cafes, often run by friends and families, have become the speciality Rebel Alliance taking on the Empire of commodity coffee culture.

To stay ahead of the game, indie cafes are constantly skilling up and improving their offer, as well as working more closely with the roasteries that ethically source and carefully bronze the beans.

'When we started, 11 years ago, the industry was full of secrets and baristas were too afraid to adjust their own grinders and machines. Crazy! We knew that sharing knowledge and empowering baristas would mean better coffee and happier customers. Today, quality and knowledge are more accessible than ever,' says David Faulkner of Bristol's Extract Coffee Roasters.

While the number of speciality set-ups has continued to rise and put pressure on the big brands, the chains aren't ready to give up any territory. Their quick adoption of speciality spiel such as 'flat white', 'cold brew' and 'single origin' suggests they're hot on the heels of the indies, while Coca-Cola's £3.9bn investment in Costa in August 2018 signals things are hotting up further.

'Predicting how this is going to affect the indie coffee market depends on the direction which Coca-Cola want to drive Costa forward,' says Dave Stanton of Exeter's Crankhouse Coffee.

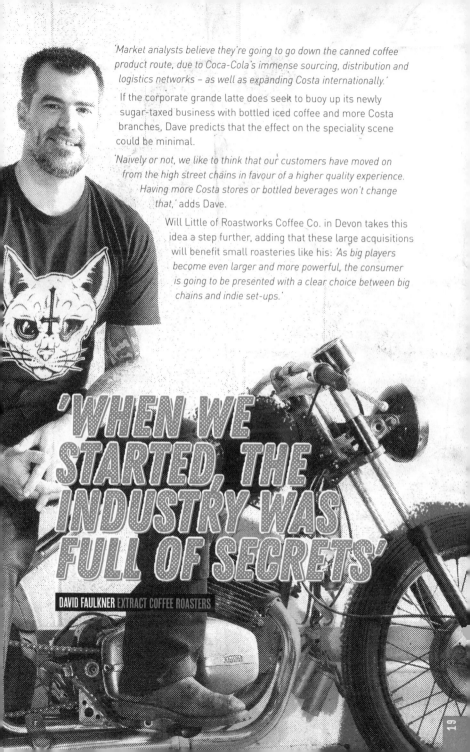

'Market analysts believe they're going to go down the canned coffee product route, due to Coca-Cola's immense sourcing, distribution and logistics networks – as well as expanding Costa internationally.'

If the corporate grande latte does seek to buoy up its newly sugar-taxed business with bottled iced coffee and more Costa branches, Dave predicts that the effect on the speciality scene could be minimal.

'Naively or not, we like to think that our customers have moved on from the high street chains in favour of a higher quality experience. Having more Costa stores or bottled beverages won't change that,' adds Dave.

Will Little of Roastworks Coffee Co. in Devon takes this idea a step further, adding that these large acquisitions will benefit small roasteries like his: 'As big players become even larger and more powerful, the consumer is going to be presented with a clear choice between big chains and indie set-ups.'

'WHEN WE STARTED, THE INDUSTRY WAS FULL OF SECRETS'

DAVID FAULKNER EXTRACT COFFEE ROASTERS

19

GROWING PAINS

As the coffee corporations continue to grow, so do the indies and a new league of boutique speciality chains has cropped up across the country. Whereas a decade ago indie coffee ventures catered to a niche audience, speciality's explosion has led to an increase in the volume of venues, which includes a crop of successful set-ups launching sister stores to meet the demand for their creative concept.

'We're seeing more coffee shops opening second sites and then turning to roasting,' says James Shepherd of the Specialty Coffee Association (SCA). *'The indie roasteries are also expanding their production and moving on to bigger roasters as demand increases. Next, I think we'll see more roasters owning coffee farmland at origin.'*

While the expansion of independently owned cafes and roasteries is fantastic news for small businesses and consumers (who will find it even easier to get their hands on a cracking cup), some die-hard coffee geeks have sniffed at the success of small-scale speciality cafe groups.

'Regardless of whether venues are one-off independent coffee shops or part of an independent group, if they're pushing the speciality coffee industry forward and doing a good job of it, they should be celebrated,' asserts David Faulkner.

The important thing is that the indie scene works together, not against itself – and that includes on the roasting side, too. Roaster Will Little says: *'The rise in multi-site cafe chains turning to roasting could become an issue for some large speciality roasters at first. Eventually though, as the market evolves, I think there'll be enough business to go around.'*

'THE RISE IN CAFE CHAINS TURNING TO ROASTING COULD BE AN ISSUE'

WILL LITTLE ROASTWORKS COFFEE CO.

VERY GREEN BEANS

In many ways the speciality sector has been at the vanguard of eco-awareness within the hospitality industry. Building on speciality's roots in sustainable bean sourcing and ethical practices, cafe owners and roasteries were ditching disposable cups, using compostables, adopting sustainable activities and reducing waste long before David Attenborough brought plastics to the attention of the masses in BBC One's *Blue Planet II*.

While coffee shops have encouraged their customers to champion the KeepCup for years, Boston Tea Party stepped up the green game in spring 2018 by introducing a blanket ban on single-use cups at its 22 cafes. Within six weeks it had saved a Transit-van-sized load of disposables from heading to landfill – and indie coffee shops across the UK are beginning to follow suit.

Roasteries are also doing their bit for the planet. Yallah Coffee in Cornwall and Extract Coffee Roasters are both using waste coffee grounds and chaff from the roasting process to produce biofuels to keep their roasteries ticking over.

While things are heading in the right direction, *the coffee industry is still at the start of its sustainable journey,* says Richard Blake, founder of Yallah.

We've been doing some research into energy efficiency and were surprised to find that, taking everything (including growing, shipping and roasting) into account, often over 50 per cent of coffee's carbon emissions are produced in the cafe.

A large part of this comes from heating and building efficiency (most cafes keep their doors open) and espresso machines also play a big part. We're stressing to our customers that recycling is great but it's also worth being mindful about the efficiency of your machine.

Consumers are becoming more savvy, however, so demand for sustainable products is increasing at both roaster and cafe level. Hopefully, this will inspire the industry to push further for a sustainable future.

NKS

DONUTS

'50 PER CENT OF COFFEE'S CARBON EMISSIONS ARE PRODUCED IN THE CAFE'

RICHARD BLAKE **YALLAH COFFEE**

'ALL OF OUR COFFEES ARE GROWN AND ROASTED BY WOMEN'

FI O'BRIEN AND CASEY LALONDE **GIRLS WHO GRIND**

GIRL POWER

In the last year, we've not only seen the first female World Barista Champion crowned, we've also watched as female coffee farmers and girl power roasters have received some serious airtime.

'The industry has changed considerably since I started out as a barista,' says Agnieszka Rojewska, 2018 World Barista Champion. 'I was ecstatic to win the WBC, but of course anyone would feel like this, regardless of gender. It's a delicate subject but I know in some countries, especially at origin, there are serious issues regarding equality.'

Two women at the forefront of the South West's female coffee force are Fi O'Brien and Casey Lalonde of Wiltshire's Girls Who Grind. Wanting to offer an alternative in the male dominated coffee industry, the dynamic duo are representing the women who keep the coffee crops flourishing.

'It's not just the taste of the coffee that's important to us but also the stories behind it,' says Fi. 'Women make up over 50 per cent of the coffee farming workforce but are often under-appreciated and underpaid.'

'All of our coffees are grown and roasted by women; we're here to big up the incredible ladies in the coffee industry,' adds Casey.

Happily it's not just this all-female Wiltshire roastery putting gender on the agenda. '2018 has been a great year for women in coffee,' says David of Extract. '80 per cent of Extract's coffee is roasted by women so it's encouraging to see the rest of the industry adopting a more equal way of working.'

GRUB'S UP

Long gone are the days when the best match for your flattie was a limp almond croissant, desert-dry muffin or burnt-to-a-crisp panini. The indie cafe scene has seriously upped the game when it comes to perfect pairings for expertly crafted coffee – and it's fuelling the flames of an innovative fast-casual dining movement.

Indie cafe owners know that flat whites and traybakes alone won't pay the rent, so they've embraced the serving of simple but delicious, freshly made food to complement the bill of quality drinks.

From breakfast to brunch to afternoon bakes and cakes, you're pretty much guaranteed to eat well (and ethically) at speciality coffee shops. The SCA's James Shepherd thinks that antipodean culture is an influence: 'The brunch market in speciality hotspots such as Melbourne is huge and [UK] cafe owners have taken inspiration from their pared-back menus.'

Paying the same attention to sourcing, sustainability and quality of the food that they apply to coffee, speciality cafe owners champion local producers and seasonal crops in dishes that are fresh, unprocessed and unpretentious – while often being pretty indulgent, too.

In the same way that some cafe owners are exerting control over the quality of the coffee they serve by roasting it in-house, they're also increasingly producing their own sourdough bread alongside the homemade cakes. The sweet result is the burgeoning cafe bakery trend.

Getting creative with preserving, curing and fermenting is also on the up. 'They want to take more of the chain into their own hands – from farm to cup and field to plate,' asserts James.

'Some of the most exciting food in the UK and Ireland at the moment is appearing on all-day brunch menus or served at cafe supper clubs and pop-up events.'

'SOME OF THE MOST EXCITING FOOD IN THE UK AND IRELAND IS APPEARING ON ALL-DAY BUNCH MENUS OR SERVED AT CAFE SUPPER CLUBS'

JAMES SHEPHERD SCA

PGS (Perfect Grinding System) integrated management system.

For the highest quality coffee and the greatest possible flexibility.

Customisable 4.3" touch screen display.

To create a set of custom settings every time.

Compact design and hopper with smart shape.

To improve visibility from the counter and simplify refill and cleaning.

Work cycle integrated with Inverter motor.

To ensure low consumption and constant performance.

New LaCimbali Elective

PERFECT COFFEE STARTS THIS WAY.

The quality of a coffee is never just about the bean.
It's never just about the roasting process, and neither is it ever just about that first sip.
The perfect coffee is an idea in constant evolution.
Welcome to the world of **Elective**.

M100 HD

Inspired by the Future

 Integral HD Pressure Profiling System
for direct control at any point during the extraction process.

 Touchscreen control
for 'On the fly' pressure profiling and setting control.

 Independent group boilers
for complete temperature control.

 TurboSteam Milk4
for increased productivity and complete milk control.

HOW TO USE THE GUIDE

№33

THE EPIPHANY @ RWA

CAFES

Coffee shops and cafes where you can drink top-notch speciality coffee. We've split the guide into areas to help you find places near you.

ROASTERS

Meet the leading speciality coffee roasters in the South West and South Wales and discover where to source beans. Find them after the cafes in each area.

MAPS

Every cafe and roastery has a number so you can find them either on the area map at the start of each section, or on the detailed city maps.

MORE GOOD STUFF

Discover **MORE GOOD CUPS** and **MORE GOOD ROASTERS** at the back of the book.

Don't forget to let us know how you get on as you explore the best speciality cafes and roasteries.

WWW.INDYCOFFEE.GUIDE

🐦 @indycoffeeguide 📷 @indycoffeeguide

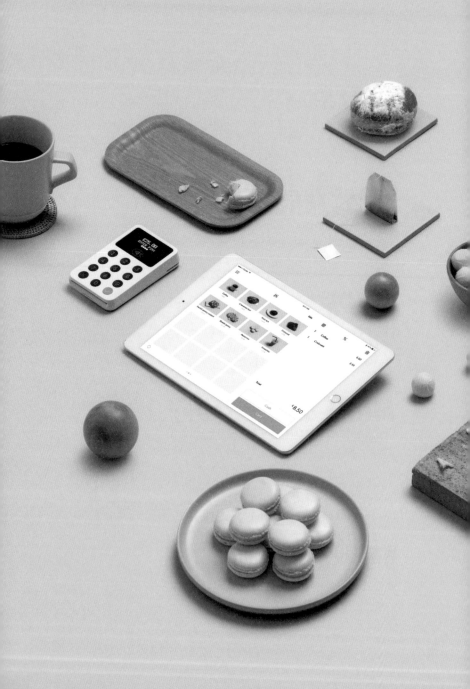

Tools to run your coffee shop

iZettle

izettle.com/indycoffeeguide

YOUR
ADVEN-
TURE

STARTS
HERE

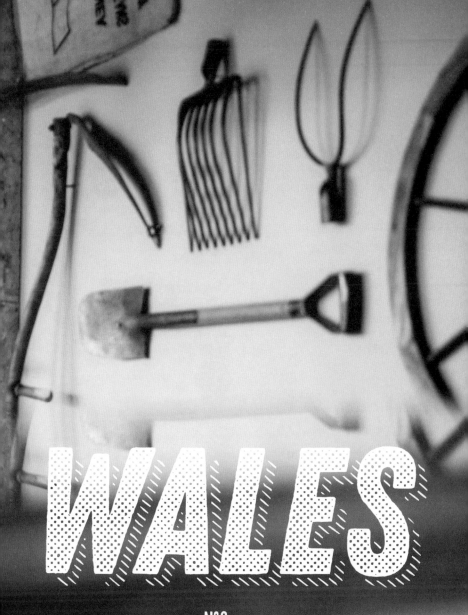

WALES

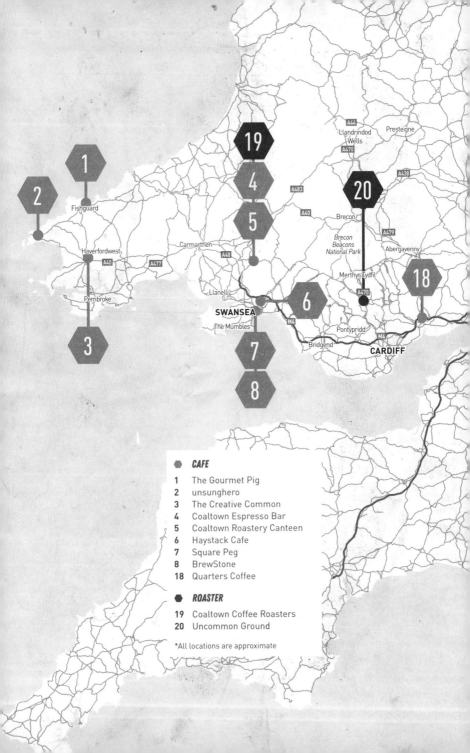

CAFE

1 The Gourmet Pig
2 unsunghero
3 The Creative Common
4 Coaltown Espresso Bar
5 Coaltown Roastery Canteen
6 Haystack Cafe
7 Square Peg
8 BrewStone
18 Quarters Coffee

ROASTER

19 Coaltown Coffee Roasters
20 Uncommon Ground

*All locations are approximate

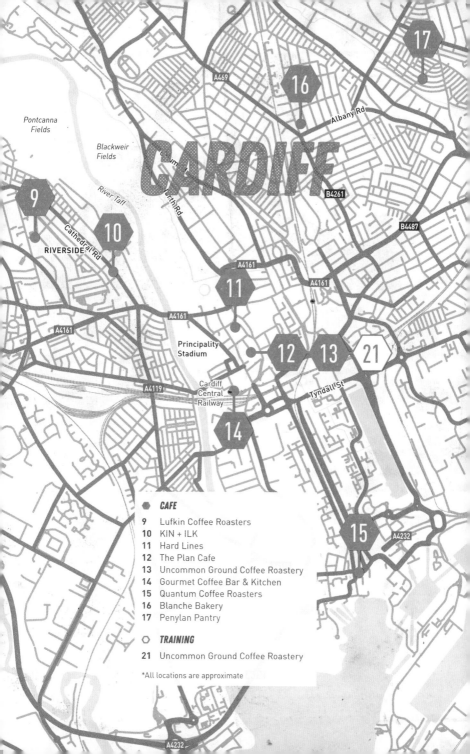

CARDIFF

CAFE

9 Lufkin Coffee Roasters
10 KIN + ILK
11 Hard Lines
12 The Plan Cafe
13 Uncommon Ground Coffee Roastery
14 Gourmet Coffee Bar & Kitchen
15 Quantum Coffee Roasters
16 Blanche Bakery
17 Penylan Pantry

TRAINING

21 Uncommon Ground Coffee Roastery

*All locations are approximate

MAP Nº 1 THE GOURMET PIG

32 West Street, Fishguard, Pembrokeshire, SA65 9AD

From its corner location a brief totter from the sea, The Gourmet Pig is a unique – and welcome – find in tiny Fishguard. Committed to Welsh produce (and more specifically to food from Pembrokeshire) the friendly deli is packed to the gunwales with artisanal delights from the Pig's doorstep.

Heady notes of coffee, ground and brewed by the Mazzer and La Marzocco, draw in locals and vacationers alike. House blend beans find their way from The Roastery in Clapham, with South Wales' Coaltown Coffee taking guest turns. You can enjoy your brew in the industrial-chic cafe area with its galvanised-sheet walls and upcycled wooden benches, or choose a seat outside and sip your perfectly poured latte while watching the holiday crowd head to the coast.

INSIDER'S TIP MUSTER THE ENERGY FOR A COASTAL STOMP BY KICKING OFF WITH THE WEEKEND COOKED BRUNCH

Pair your pick with delicious edibles: bulging sandwiches overflowing with fillings including local ham, blue cheese and crab meat; and deli boards featuring locally cured charcuterie. Then follow with a slice of homemade bara brith for a fruity treat steeped in tradition.

ESTABLISHED
2009

KEY ROASTER
The Roastery

BREWING METHOD
Espresso

MACHINE
La Marzocco

GRINDER
Mazzer

OPENING HOURS
Mon-Thu **9.30**am-**5.30**pm
Fri **9.30**am-**6.30**pm
Sat **9.30**am-**4.30**pm
Sun **10**am-**4**pm

 Gluten FREE

 BEANS AVAILABLE INSTORE

 WIFI

 CYCLE FRIENDLY

 OUTDOOR seating

 FAMILY FRIENDLY

 DISABLED ACCESS

 BRING YOUR OWN Cup

---

www.gourmetpig.co.uk   T: 01348 874404

f @gourmetpig   🐦 @gourmetpig   📷 @thegourmetpig

MAP 2 UNSUNGHERO

28a High Street, St Davids, Pembrokeshire, SA62 6SD

The unsungheroes live by the holy trinity of surf, skate and coffee.

By the team's own admission, folk don't expect to roll into a boutique surf shop to be greeted by the olfactory onslaught of freshly ground beans. Yet St Davids' visiting surfers and skaters follow their noses (and the locals) to the tiny city's best cup – served with a side of board wax, wheels and wetsuits.

The espresso needed to fuel coastal exploits is knocked up by knowledgeable baristas, and showcases a regularly changing line-up of single origins and blends from roasters including Square Mile, James Gourmet and Extract.

TIP CHECK OUT THE ART ON DISPLAY ALONGSIDE HIGH-IMPACT SKATE GRAPHICS

Browse the carefully selected range of surf and skate gear while you sip, before venturing to the 'Skate Cave' in the basement to swoon over a display of eye-popping decks.

If you shudder at the thought of yourself in a wetsuit or pulling a 360, stick to browsing the coffee kit instead: beans and pourover gear are all available to take away.

ESTABLISHED
2013

KEY ROASTER
Multiple roasters

BREWING METHOD
Espresso

MACHINE
Fracino Classic

GRINDER
Mahlkonig K30

OPENING HOURS
Mon-Sun 9am-5pm

BEANS AVAILABLE INSTORE

WIFI

www.unsungherosurf.co.uk   T: 01437 729437

f @unsungherosurf   🐦 @unsungherosurf   📷 @unsungherosurf

™ 3 THE CREATIVE COMMON

The Old Coach House, Goat Street, Haverfordwest, Pembrokeshire, SA61 1PX

It didn't take long for the bright sparks behind community co-working space The Creative Common to see the potential to indulge their passion for quality coffee while simultaneously fuelling their crowd of keyboard warriors. And so the in-house cafe was born.

The team enlisted the help of local roastery Capital to craft a luscious house blend, which is supplemented by a regularly changing seasonal single origin from Bristol's Clifton Coffee.

TIP ROCK UP ON A FRIDAY FOR THE BEST BACON ROLL IN TOWN

Espresso, cold brew and filter thrills are often extended after hours thanks to a lively line-up of events which covers everything from ring carving workshops to surf exhibitions. There are also regular bar evenings and next year sees the launch of The Common's first pale ale in collaboration with local brewery Triple D.

Improving the coastal hangout's eco credentials has been high on the agenda this year – check out the range of refashioned coffee-grounds products which include scrub soap and firelighters.

ESTABLISHED
2016

KEY ROASTER
Capital Roasters

BREWING METHOD
Espresso, V60,
AeroPress,
Chemex,
Clever Dripper,
cold brew

MACHINE
Fracino
Bambino

GRINDER
Fracino

OPENING HOURS
Mon-Fri **8**am-**3**pm
(extended in summer)

  Gluten FREE

 BEANS AVAILABLE INSTORE

 WIFI

 CYCLE FRIENDLY

 OUTDOOR SEATING

 DISABLED ACCESS

 BRING YOUR OWN Cup

---

www.thecreativecommon.co.uk T: 01437 779397

f @thecreativecommon @ @thecreativecommon

MAP No 4 COALTOWN ESPRESSO BAR

4 The Arcade, College Street, Ammanford, Carmarthenshire, SA18 2LN

A rural ex-mining town isn't the first place you'd expect to find a beautifully designed espresso bar serving single origin coffee, yet Ammanford is enjoying a slice of the speciality action thanks to Coaltown.

Setting up the Carmarthenshire coffee roastery in 2014, the Coaltown team are as passionate about creating jobs in their hometown as they are about roasting lip-smacking beans. The petite coffee shop within the Victorian arcade was the second step in their grand plan and the third is the new roastery, training space and cafe on the outskirts of Ammanford which launched late 2018.

INSIDER'S TIP BRING YOUR PHONE, THIS IS FULL-ON INSTAGRAM TERRITORY

Considering its size, the tiny space on College Street houses a surprisingly vast selection of coffees from its home roastery. Ask the barista for the latest tasting notes and best serve style, then buy a bag of your favourite beans to take home.

If you can't find a seat among the locals, head across town to the roastery HQ where the Coaltown crew sling flat whites alongside a stonking bill of brunch dishes.

ESTABLISHED
2018

KEY ROASTER
Coaltown Coffee Roasters

BREWING METHOD
Espresso, V60, Chemex

MACHINE
La Marzocco Linea PB

GRINDER
Victoria Arduino Mythos One, Mahlkonig EK43

OPENING HOURS
Mon-Fri 8am-5.30pm
Sat 9am-5.30pm
Sun 10am-4.30pm

www.coaltowncoffee.co.uk T: 01269 400105

@coaltowncoffee @coaltowncoffee

43

MAP 5 COALTOWN ROASTERY CANTEEN

Coaltown Roastery, Foundry Road, Ammanford, Carmarthenshire, SA18 2LS

Coaltown's spanking new HQ on the outskirts of Ammanford is shaking up the coffee scene in South Wales.

The family business launched its exciting second incarnation of the roastery in November 2018 and has created a speciality hub where baristas travel to learn their trade, mums congregate to chat over brunch and locals pause to pick up a bag of beans.

The huge space – furnished with houseplants, retired school chairs and design-centric machinery – on the outskirts of the ex-mining town is a melting pot of coffee culture. An espresso bar, canteen, training school and roastery all co-exist under one roof.

TIP HEAD ACROSS TOWN TO THE ESPRESSO BAR AT THE ARCADE FOR A SECOND COALTOWN SERVING

Earmark a couple of hours so you can sample the latest single origin via Chemex, tuck into one of the flatbreads fresh from the wood-fired oven and watch the roasters bronze the next batch of greens.

Check social media before you go so you can work your visit around one of the regular public cupping sessions.

ESTABLISHED
2014

KEY ROASTER
Coaltown Coffee Roasters

BREWING METHOD
Espresso, V60, Kalita Wave, Chemex

MACHINE
Modbar Espresso AV

GRINDER
Mythos One Clima Pro, Mahlkonig EK43

OPENING HOURS
Mon-Fri 8am-8pm
Sat 9am-8pm
Sun 9am-5pm

 Gluten FREE

 BEANS AVAILABLE INSTORE

 WIFI

 CYCLE FRIENDLY

 FAMILY FRIENDLY

 DISABLED ACCESS

 BRING YOUR OWN Cup

 COFFEE COURSES

---

www.coaltowncoffee.co.uk   T: 01269 400105

f @coaltowncoffeeroasters   🐦 @coaltowncoffee   📷 @coaltowncoffee

MAP 6 HAYSTACK CAFE

1 Brynhyfryd Square, Brynhyfryd, Swansea, SA5 9EB

With its 20ft mural stating *'All you need is coffee and brunch'*, this fresher on the Swansea speciality scene is pretty hard to miss.

Haystack owners Liam and Beth secured the sweet corner spot in spring 2018 and took inspiration from Beth's rural upbringing to create a sociable cafe space serving the best of South Wales' produce.

Brunch is a big deal here and house favourites such as the Haystack (hash browns, bacon, halloumi and avocado) and Farmers' Breakfast (the full brekkie bill served in a skillet pan) are packed with as many locally sourced lovelies as possible.

TIP ALMOST EVERYTHING ON THE MENU IS SOURCED FROM WITHIN AN HOUR'S DRIVE OF THE CAFE

Spending time in London before returning to Swansea, Beth and Liam wanted to pair their epic brunch offering with city-standard coffee. Happily, the locally roasted Coaltown Coffee beans provide the perfect blend of third-wave quality and Welsh locality.

Sip a coconut milk piccolo (the locals' fave) on a Chesterfield in front of the original fireplace, grab a stool at the window bar or nab one of the upcycled fence-post tables dotted around the cosy space.

ESTABLISHED
2018

KEY ROASTER
Coaltown Coffee Roasters

BREWING METHOD
Espresso, Chemex

MACHINE
La Marzocco Linea PB

GRINDER
Mahlkonig K30 Twin

OPENING HOURS
Tue-Fri 8am-5pm
Sat 9am-4pm
Sun 10am-3pm

 Gluten FREE

 WIFI

 CYCLE FRIENDLY

 OUTDOOR seating

 FAMILY friendly

DISABLED ACCESS

 BRING YOUR OWN Cup

www.haystackcafe.com   T: 07969 300110

f @haystackcafeswansea @ @haystackcafe

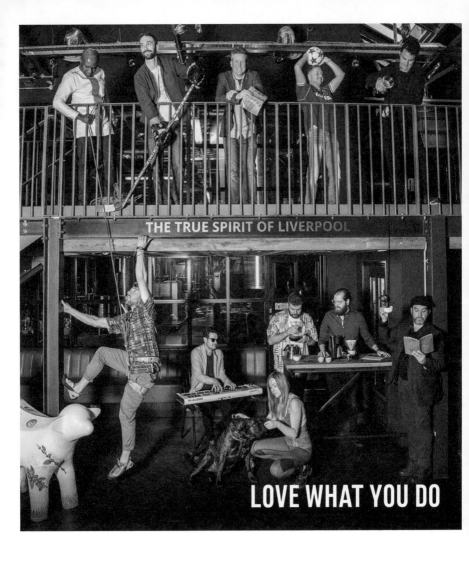

THE TRUE SPIRIT OF LIVERPOOL

LOVE WHAT YOU DO

Olam
Specialty
Coffee

New Name. Same Faces. More great coffee.

MAP 7 SQUARE PEG

29b Gower Road, Sketty, Swansea, SA2 9BX

S quare Peg introduced many of Swansea's coffee fans to speciality back in 2015 and this year the social enterprise and community cafe is teaching them how to do it for themselves via a new bill of SCA barista classes.

Between running a busy coffee shop, giving away profits to charitable causes in Swansea and Kenya, and hosting a line-up of events at the sociable space, founder Matt Crome has found time to get his AST certificate. Now he can train a whole new league of espresso slingers.

TIP MINI-PEGGERS GET THEIR OWN FOOD MENU WHICH INCLUDES PB AND BLACKBERRY TOAST

If you'd rather leave the latte art to the pros, the popular venue serves a cracking cup of Clifton Coffee, with guest beans from roasting greats such as Round Hill available on a second grinder.

We'd recommend sinking into one of the comfy sofas with your coffee of choice before chowing down on an epic Peg taco: the aloo gobi, mango, yogurt and sriracha combo is particularly messy (and all the more delicious for it).

ESTABLISHED
2015

KEY ROASTER
Clifton Coffee Roasters

BREWING METHOD
Espresso, V60, batch brew, AeroPress, cold brew

MACHINE
La Marzocco Linea PB

GRINDER
Mythos One, Mahlkonig EK43

OPENING HOURS
Mon-Sat **8**am-**5**pm

 Gluten FREE

 BEANS AVAILABLE INSTORE

 WIFI

 OUTDOOR Seating

FAMILY FRiENdly

 DISABLED ACCESS

 BRING YOUR OWN Cup

 COFFEE COURSES

www.squarepeg.org.uk T: 01792 206593

f @squarepegcoffee   @squarepegcoffee   @squarepegcoffee

MAP 8 BREWSTONE

33 Uplands Crescent, Swansea, SA2 0NP

You'll want to schedule a lunchtime stop at this sociable spot as, post midday, the intoxicating scent of freshly pulled espresso flirts with the waft of bronzing pizzas at Brewstone.

It's not just hand-stretched dough baked in the wood fired oven that seduces the senses. A feast of flame-licked wraps, small plates and skillets – think 12 hour barbecue pork; spiced aubergine with minted yogurt; and lamb kibbeh salad – satisfy foodie cravings 'til late at the cafe-restaurant-bar hybrid.

TIP VENTURE TO THE BREWSTONE BAR NEXT DOOR FOR COCKTAILS AND CRAFT BEER

Post-feed pick-me-ups come in the form of Clifton Coffee's seasonal single origin beans which are served as espresso or shaken with tequila, rum liqueur and vanilla bitters in the house martini. If your caffeine capacity has peaked, a hefty selection of Canton loose-leaf teas offers cold- and hot-brewed herbal alternatives.

Early starts, late openings and a rabbit-warren of different dining spaces means a pit stop at this Uplands fave can slot into the busiest of caffeinated road-trip schedules.

ESTABLISHED
2014

KEY ROASTER
Clifton Coffee Roasters

BREWING METHOD
Espresso, filter

MACHINE
La Spaziale Caffé d'autore

GRINDER
Compak

OPENING HOURS
Mon-Sun
7am-11pm (restaurant)
5pm-1am (bar)

 Gluten FREE

 BEANS AVAILABLE INSTORE

 WIFI

 OUTDOOR seating

 FAMILY FRIENDLY

---

www.brewstone.co.uk   T: 01792 470480

f @brewstoneswansea   🐦 @brewstoneswan   📷 @brewstone_uplands

MAP № 9 LUFKIN COFFEE ROASTERS

Kings Road Yard, 183a Kings Road, Cardiff, CF11 9DF

Leave Cardiff city centre, nip along a couple of back streets, turn down a lane by a church and land in a sunshiney yard. Possibly an offbeat location in which to find a bunch of Cali-inspired caffeine fanatics, but Lufkin has no problem drawing in like-minded locals.

Knowledge and enthusiasm for their art is in no short supply from the Lufkin crew. Not that they'll be bothering you – they also believe that enjoying a well-made brew should be a contemplative time-out savoured in relaxing surrounds.

TIP CUP ENVY? PICK UP LUFKIN'S HAND-THROWN CERAMICS FROM THE RETAIL COLLECTION

On Tuesdays the team secrete themselves in their roastery, mindfully tickling every last drop of depth and flavour from their carefully selected beans. The regularly rotating selection of brews is traceable back to the farm, and flavours are profiled and balanced to draw out the greens' exotic origins.

Love what you taste? Own-roasted beans are available to buy on-site, alongside a selection of locally made, hand-thrown ceramics as used in the coffee bar.

ESTABLISHED
2015

KEY ROASTER
Lufkin Coffee Roasters

BREWING METHOD
Espresso, drip filter, batch brew, cold brew

MACHINE
La Marzocco Linea PB

GRINDER
Mazzer Luigi, Mahlkonig EK43

OPENING HOURS
Wed-Mon 9.30am-4.30pm

 Gluten FREE

 BEANS AVAILABLE INSTORE

 WIFI

 CYCLE FRIENDLY

 OUTDOOR seating

 FAMILY FRIENDLY

 DISABLED ACCESS

 BRING YOUR OWN Cup

 COFFEE COURSES

www.lufkincoffee.com
f @lufkincoffee 🐦 @lufkincoffee 📷 @lufkincoffee

MAP № 10 KIN + ILK

31 Cathedral Road, Pontcanna, Cardiff, CF11 9HB

The clue is in the name at KIN + ILK, Cardiff's community-focused cafe on Cathedral Road.

It's where staff and customers gather together in a (metaphorical) group hug to share their love of exceptional coffee.

TIP FREE COFFEE TASTING EVENTS PROVIDE THE CHANCE TO PICK THE BRAINS OF ROASTING PROS

Direct trade with producers is important to KIN + ILK's head of coffee, James, who recently travelled to El Salvador with Clifton Coffee Roasters to seek out the best beans for the two cafes. The result is house espresso Finca El Corozo, which is grown by Fernando Lima. It's a versatile coffee which works as well black as with milk – and is served as espresso alongside a regularly updated guest on V60 and batch filter.

Brunch at KIN + ILK is a relaxed affair, and the surroundings – all twinkly lights and blonde wood – add a dash of west-coast cool to the proceedings. Dishes channel a Middle Eastern vibe, with turmeric scramble and smashed avo a fave. Pair your morning flat white with Turkish eggs and it'll see you through to supper.

ESTABLISHED
2016

KEY ROASTER
Clifton Coffee Roasters

BREWING METHOD
Espresso, V60, batch filter

MACHINE
La Marzocco Linea PB

GRINDER
Mythos One Clima Pro

OPENING HOURS
Mon-Fri 8am-6pm
Sat-Sun 9am-5pm

 Gluten FREE

 BEANS AVAILABLE INSTORE

 WIFI

 CYCLE FRIENDLY

 OUTDOOR seating

 FAMILY FRIENDLY

 DISABLED ACCESS

 BRING YOUR OWN cup

 COFFEE COURSES

www.kinandilk.com   T: 02920 789842

f @kinandilk   🐦 @kinandilkpc   📷 @kinandilk

MAP №11 HARD LINES

Unit 25, Cardiff Central Market, St Mary Street, Cardiff, CF10 1AU

It's been a busy first year at Cardiff's smallest speciality coffee shop. The new venue from the Hard Lines team was an instant hit when it opened in 2017 and the Cardiff Indoor Market espresso bar is regularly mobbed by coffee fans brandishing KeepCups.

The Barb house special (a mix of beetroot and spices) earned the team some serious airtime on social – so much so that the fuchsia latte has secured a permanent spot on the drinks menu.

TIP LOOK OUT FOR AN EXCITING NEW VENTURE LAUNCHING IN 2019

The creative gang also started roasting their own coffee this year and already stock a number of shops in the capital – alongside the Hard Lines gaff – with single origin beans.

Roasting takes place nearby on a weekly basis so get your orders in online or in-store if you want to get nab a bag. You'll also find team Hard Lines flogging beans and slinging espresso at Riverside Farmers Market every Sunday from nine 'til two.

ESTABLISHED
2016

KEY ROASTER
Hard Lines
Coffee

BREWING METHOD
Espresso, filter,
batch brew,
cold brew

MACHINE
La Marzocco
Linea Classic

GRINDER
Mythos One,
Mahlkonig EK43

OPENING HOURS
Mon-Fri 8am-5pm
Sat 9am-5pm

www.hard-lines.co.uk   T: 07428 695997

f @hardlinescoffee   🐦 @hardlinescoffee   📷 @hardlinescoffee

MAP 12 THE PLAN CAFE

28-29 Morgan Arcade, Cardiff, CF10 1AF

Serving quality coffee since 2002, The Plan was one of the original pioneers of the Welsh speciality scene.

Head barista Trevor Hyam has led the busy bar at the heart of Morgan Arcade cafe for over a decade and continues to champion expertly prepared coffee, passing on skills to his small team of passionate baristas.

Alongside espresso, the traditional set-up welcomes two to three single origin coffees from James Gourmet each week prepared on french press, along with a batch brew option from Union. In summer, there's also homemade cold brew for post-shopping refreshment, as well as freshly blitzed smoothies and organic milkshakes.

TIP THE PLAN WAS INCLUDED IN THE SUNDAY TIMES TOP 25 COFFEE SHOPS

A unique hexagonal design means there are plenty of window spots from which to watch passersby weave through the Victorian arcade – if you can't find a seat downstairs, there are additional tables on the mezzanine level.

Wherever you settle, we recommend taking your time over Trevor's seasonal pick on espresso as you peruse the breakfast, brunch and lunch offerings.

ESTABLISHED
2002

KEY ROASTER
James Gourmet
Coffee

BREWING METHOD
Espresso, cold brew,
french press,
batch brew

MACHINE
Astoria Plus 4 You

GRINDER
Anfim Super
Caimano

OPENING HOURS
Mon-Sat **8.45**am-**5**pm
Sun **10**am-**4**pm

Gluten FREE

BEANS AVAILABLE INSTORE

WIFI

OUTDOOR seating

FAMILY FRIENDLY

---

www.theplancafecardiff.co.uk T: 02920 398764

f @theplancafecardiff 🐦 @theplancafe

MAP №13 UNCOMMON GROUND COFFEE ROASTERY

10-12 Royal Arcade, Cardiff, CF10 1AE

This family-run coffee shop was an instant hit with Cardiff's speciality-savvy sippers when brothers Paul and Ian Hayman set up in Royal Arcade in 2015.

Almost four years on and the moodily lit hangout is even busier (if that's possible) and now proudly serves its own-roasted beans to the fans who throng the antique tables.

Newbies pitching up at the sociable space are advised to ease in with the Uncommon house-blend flat white before exploring the single origin options on pourover, AeroPress or batch brew.

INSIDERS TIP SIGN UP FOR A COFFEE COURSE IN THE UNCOMMON ROOM EVENTS SPACE

In summer, we'd recommend picking up a bottle of cold brew and a slice of cake and heading to nearby Bute Park.

While the focus here is coffee, you'll find an inviting menu of snacks, sandwiches and homemade deliciousness. Also fresh and fabulous is the new vegan superfood bowl – a colourful collision of good-for-the-soul fodder.

ESTABLISHED
2015

KEY ROASTER
Uncommon Ground

BREWING METHOD
Espresso, V60, cold brew, batch brew, AeroPress,

MACHINE
La Spaziale

GRINDER
Anfim Caimano OD

OPENING HOURS
Mon-Sat 7.30am-6.30pm
Sun 10am-5.30pm

 Gluten FREE

 BEANS AVAILABLE INSTORE

 WIFI

 CYCLE FRIENDLY

 OUTDOOR SEATING

 FAMILY FRIENDLY

 BRING YOUR OWN CUP

 COFFEE COURSES

www.uncommon-ground.co.uk   T: 02920 224236
f @uncommongroundcoffeeroastery   🐦 @_uncommonground   📷 @_uncommonground

RAISE YOUR COFFEE GAME

ROASTWORKS®
COFFEE C^o LTD

INSTAGRAM.COM/ROASTWORKS_COFFEE_CO
@ROASTWORKSDEVON
FB.COM/ROASTWORKSCOFFEECO
ROASTWORKS.CO.UK

MAP№ 14 GOURMET COFFEE BAR & KITCHEN

Central Square, Cardiff, CF10 1EP

T ransport hubs have a rep for bad coffee but Gourmet Coffee Bar is stopping the trend in its tracks at Cardiff's Central and Queen Street train stations.

Serving Union espresso and single origin batch brew to weary commuters and jaded day trippers, the micro-coffee shops are turning South Wales' workforce to the speciality stuff – one velvety flat white and fruity filter at a time.

TIP HEADING NORTH? FIND GCB'S SISTER OUTLET AT WREXHAM TRAIN STATION

The team's drive to get the nation quaffing quality caffeine doesn't stop at the bottom of a KeepCup though: retail bags of Union's seasonal single estate beans and Revelation house espresso blend are on sale so customers' standards don't slip when they get home.

On-the-go foodie thrills at the coffee bars consist of a short but sweet bill of soups, sandwiches, wraps, cakes and traybakes. There's also a selection of banging loose-leaf blends from Brew Tea Co if you've timetabled a snooze for the journey.

ESTABLISHED
2016

KEY ROASTER
Union Hand-Roasted Coffee

BREWING METHOD
Espresso, batch brew

MACHINE
La Marzocco Linea Classic

GRINDER
Mazzer Major

OPENING HOURS
Mon-Fri 6am-7pm
Sun 7am-5pm

Gluten FREE

BEANS AVAILABLE INSTORE

WIFI

CYCLE FRIENDLY

OUTDOOR SEATING

DISABLED ACCESS

---

www.gourmetcoffeebar.co.uk T: 01978 660700

🐦 @gourmetcbandk 📷 @gourmetcoffeebar

MAP № 15 QUANTUM COFFEE ROASTERS

58 Bute Street, Butetown, Cardiff, CF10 5BN

While baristas are becoming ever more knowledgeable, opportunities to quiz the roaster on the origin of the beans and flavour profiles while you sip are still rather rare – unless you get your daily fix at Quantum.

Owners, roasters and part-time baristas Katia and Dimitri spend as much time as possible behind the bar of their Cardiff Bay coffee shop and say: *'Customers like that we're here almost every day and love to chat about the latest coffee.'*

TIP BAG QUANTUM ROASTED BEANS FROM THE RETAIL SHELVES TO BREW AT HOME

When the duo aren't slinging espresso, pouring V60s or getting experimental with the cold brew tower, they're down the road at the new roastery bronzing beans from up-and-coming regions such as Myanmar and Papua New Guinea.

The team at Quantum are also the local experts in Greek/Turkish coffee so expect bold flavours and experimental batches – make sure to ask for the best serve style for each bean. If you're popping by post-12pm, ask about the seasonal nitro espresso stout that's brewed in collaboration with Mad Dog.

ESTABLISHED
2015

KEY ROASTER
Quantum Coffee Roasters

BREWING METHOD
Espresso, V60, Chemex, ibrick, cold brew tower

MACHINE
Britesso

GRINDER
Iberital Santos Zara x 2

OPENING HOURS
Mon-Fri 8am-6pm
Sat 9am-6pm
Sun 10am-6pm

 Gluten FREE

 BEANS AVAILABLE INSTORE

 WIFI

 FAMILY FRIENDLY

 DISABLED ACCESS

 BRING YOUR OWN Cup

www.quantumroasters.co.uk   T: 07413 543335
f @quantumroasters   🐦 @quantumroasters   📷 @quantumroasters

MAP № 16 BLANCHE BAKERY

16 Mackintosh Place, Roath, Cardiff, CF24 4RQ

Take a scroll through Blanche's feed and you'll see why the vegan bakery and coffee shop is fast becoming one of the most Instagrammed spots in Cardiff.

Scoffing doughnuts in front of the floral wall or taking flat lay pics of perfectly poured flat whites may earn a lot of love on the 'gram for the fans who flock here, but this isn't style over substance.

INSIDER'S TIP DON'T LEAVE WITHOUT SAMPLING THE BADASS VEGAN BURGER

Founders Rem and Amy are as passionate about the Assembly coffee served at their strictly-vegan cafe as they are about delivering freshly fried dough and all-day brunch dishes.

'We dial in the espresso with each milk alternative to yield the best flavour notes,' explains Rem.

The single origin beans from the London roastery are going down a storm with oat milk as a flat white or lavished with ice and tonic. Whichever you go for, a side of beautifully decorated doughnuts is non-negotiable.

ESTABLISHED
2017

KEY ROASTER
Assembly Coffee

BREWING METHOD
Espresso,
cold brew,
batch brew,
filter

MACHINE
La Marzocco
GS3 AV

GRINDER
Mahlkonig EK43

OPENING HOURS
Thu-Mon **12**pm-**6**pm

Gluten FREE
BEANS AVAILABLE INSTORE
WIFI

BRING YOUR OWN Cup

www.blanchebakery.co.uk   T: 07806 640405

f @blanchecardiff   🐦 @blanchecardiff   📷 @blanchecardiff

MAP№ 17 PENYLAN PANTRY

72 Kimberley Road, Penylan, Cardiff, CF23 5DN

Melissa Boothman was ahead of the curve when she opened her popular Penylan delicatessen and cafe in 2013.

Launching as an environmentally-conscious concept which offered a wide range of milk alternatives at no extra cost and championing hyper-local producers from day one, the Pantry was doing the eco thing before green became the new black.

TIP DON'T SURRENDER TO YOUR USUAL ORDER 'TIL YOU'VE SURVEYED THE SEASONAL DRINKS SPECIALS

Five years on, Melissa and team have also taken their ethical ethos to the new Secret Garden Cafe within Bute Park, where they're offering a second helping of the Cardiff-roasted Hard Lines coffee and incredible homemade cakes.

However, the original neighbourhood outpost on Kimberley Road is still your go-to to stock up on Riverside sourdough, made-up-the-road preserves and coffee beans to brew at home. After you've filled your tote, stick around for an Alchemy AeroPress and rainbow bowl of goodness from the colourful seasonal salad bar.

ESTABLISHED
2013

KEY ROASTER
Multiple
roasters

BREWING METHOD
Espresso,
AeroPress,
cafetiere

MACHINE
La Spaziale
S5 Compact,
Nuova Simonelli
Aurelia II

GRINDER
Anfim SCODY,
Nuova Simonelli
Mythos One

OPENING HOURS
Tue-Sat **9**am-**6**pm
Sun **10**am-**4**pm

 Gluten FREE

 BEANS AVAILABLE INSTORE

 WIFI

 CYCLE FRIENDLY

 OUTDOOR SEATING

 DISABLED ACCESS

 BRING YOUR OWN Cup

www.penylanpantry.com

 f @penylanpantry @penylanpantry @penylanpantry

MAP 18 QUARTERS COFFEE

Unit 1, Glen Avon House, Millennium Walk, Newport, NP19 0LZ

One of the pioneering speciality purveyors in Wales' third city, Quarters Coffee answered the prayers of Newport's coffee drinkers when it opened in 2018.

While the spectacular riverside location and kick-back-and-relax atmosphere add a certain something, it's the brew that's the main draw here.

The house espresso is North Star's Brazil Fazenda Rainha Da Paz, a creamy marriage of chocolate, nut and date notes, while guest roasts (including Square Mile and Small Batch) stump up the goods for promiscuous sippers.

INSIDER TIP NAB A SEAT AT THE WINDOW AND ENJOY UNLIMITED COFFEE VIA THE FREELANCERS' DEAL

With two families at the helm, Quarters has a welcome-home feel that's amplified by the friendly staff. Creating a consistently good cup and letting the character of the beans shine through every time takes dedication, but that's what the baristas strive for.

Cakes change daily and come from Newport's small-batch Carrot Top Bakery. On sunny days (fingers crossed), take lunch on the terrace and dip into the chiller for a craft ale or cider.

ESTABLISHED
2018

KEY ROASTER
North Star
Coffee Roasters

BREWING METHOD
Espresso, V60

MACHINE
La Marzocco
Linea PB ABR

GRINDER
Fiorenzato F64
EVO, Mahlkonig
EK43

OPENING HOURS
Mon-Thu 8am-6pm
Fri 8am-11pm
Sat 9am-11pm

Gluten FREE

BEANS AVAILABLE INSTORE

WIFI

CYCLE FRIENDLY

OUTDOOR SEATING

FAMILY FRIENDLY

DISABLED ACCESS

COFFEE COURSES

www.quarterscoffee.com   T: 07920 037837

f @quarterscoffee   🐦 @quarterscoffee   📷 @quarterscoffee

SOUTH WALES ROASTERS

MAP №19 COALTOWN COFFEE ROASTERS

Foundry Road, Ammanford, Carmarthenshire, SA18 2LS

It's been an epic year for Coaltown, South Wales' pioneering coffee roasters.
Not only did Coaltown feature in *Lonely Planet*'s Global Coffee Tour as one of the top five places for coffee in the UK, the roastery also opened the doors of its new HQ on the outskirts of Ammanford.

As well as housing two Probat roasters, a dedicated cupping lab and canteen with wood-fired oven, the fresh set-up is also home to a barista academy where the Coaltown team train locals to help them gain employment with the roastery's wholesale customers. *'Our overriding purpose is to bring industry back to our ex-mining community,'* explains founder Scott James.

'COALTOWN FEATURED IN LONELY PLANET'S GLOBAL COFFEE TOUR AS ONE OF THE TOP FIVE PLACES FOR COFFEE IN THE UK'

The speciality classes ensure that all of the aspiring baristas graduate with the knowledge to knock up a cracking cup – whether they're slinging 'spros at the Coaltown espresso bar across town or one of the Welsh indie cafes which stock the award winning beans.

ESTABLISHED
2014

ROASTER
MAKE & SIZE
Probat
Probatone 12kg
Probat UG 75kg

CAFE ONSITE

OPEN TO THE PUBLIC

COFFEE COURSES

BEANS AVAILABLE
ONLINE | OUTLETS

www.coaltowncoffee.co.uk T: 01269 400105
f @coaltowncoffeeroasters @coaltowncoffee @coaltowncoffee

MAP № 20 UNCOMMON GROUND

Mid Glamorgan, South Wales

T here's usually a good story or inspiring character behind the name given to a roaster and Florence, the gleaming Diedrich that takes centre stage at Uncommon Ground's Abercynon roastery, is no exception.

It's named after roastery owners Paul and Ian Hayman's grandmother, which makes sense as family is at the very heart of this growing South Wales brand.

The brothers spend their days roasting the next batch of beans destined for their customers or for the grinders at their Cardiff arcade cafe.

ESTABLISHED
2016

ROASTER
MAKE & SIZE
Diedrich 2.5 IR

OPEN
BY APPOINTMENT

COFFEE
COURSES

BEANS
AVAILABLE
ONLINE ONSITE

'UNCOMMON GROUND HAS BECOME ONE OF THE SERIOUS CONTENDERS ON THE WELSH SPECIALITY SCENE'

Increasing their wholesale subscriptions and expanding into machine leasing and sales this year, Uncommon Ground have become one of the serious contenders on the Welsh speciality scene. Their mission remains the same however: *'Quite simply, we want to get people brewing and drinking better coffee,'* says Paul. *'Speciality shouldn't be complicated. It's an affordable luxury that should be accessible to everyone.'*

www.uncommon-ground.co.uk   T: 02920 224236

f @uncommongroundcoffeeroastery   🐦 @_uncommonground   📷 @_uncommonground

MAP № 21 UNCOMMON GROUND COFFEE ROASTERY

10-12 Royal Arcade, Cardiff, CF10 1AE

Ever picture yourself behind the bar of a coffee shop? If the answer is a resounding 'Hell, yeah!' you need to join the crowd of aspiring coffee pros living the barista dream at Uncommon Ground's after-hours training sessions.

The informal but informative classes with Uncommon's head of coffee, Dominik Hurthe, are a fantastic introduction to life on the other side of the bar.

They're also an opportunity to feel the thrill of slinging espresso and pouring latte art using the latest kit – but without the pressure of spectators.

ESTABLISHED
2016

CAFE ONSITE

COFFEE COURSES

BEANS AVAILABLE

'BUDDING BEANSMITHS CAN BRONZE THEIR OWN BLEND OF SINGLE ORIGIN BEANS TO BREW AT HOME'

Sessions cover a range of topics from basic industry barista skills to home brewing (learn how to make cracking coffee from your V60, AeroPress and cafetiere). There are also bespoke masterclasses for those who want to take their caffeine geekery to the next level.

Budding beansmiths can also enrol on the roasting course at the Uncommon Ground Roastery where they'll bronze their own blend of single origin beans to brew at home.

---

www.uncommon-ground.co.uk　T: 02920 224236

f @uncommongroundcoffeeroastery　🐦 @_uncommonground　📷 @_uncommonground

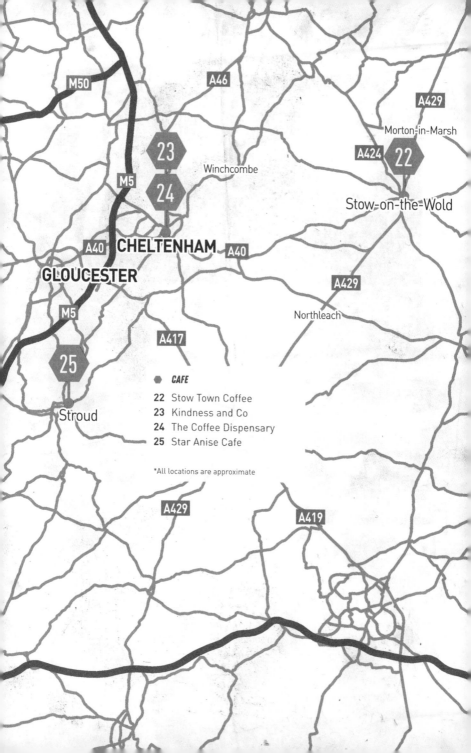

M50

A46

A429

Morton-in-Marsh

23

Winchcombe

A424 **22**

M5

24

Stow-on-the-Wold

A40 **CHELTENHAM** A40

GLOUCESTER

A429

M5

Northleach

25

A417

● *CAFE*

22 Stow Town Coffee
23 Kindness and Co
24 The Coffee Dispensary
25 Star Anise Cafe

Stroud

*All locations are approximate

A429

A419

MAP№ 22 STOW TOWN COFFEE

2 Wells Barn, Sheep Street, Stow-on-the-Wold, Gloucestershire, GL54 1AA

Having owned one of the most successful coffee shops in the Cotswolds for many years, Ali and Dave Cunliffe decided to adopt a more unique approach when setting up their new venture: a tiny coffee roastery and espresso bar nestled in the centre of Stow-on-the-Wold.

'We adored running our old place but our work-life balance was skewed to say the least,' says Ali. 'A big part of what we've always loved is talking to people about coffee, so to demonstrate how coffee is roasted and serve them a freshly ground brew at the same time is fantastic.'

TIP PAIR YOUR COFFEE WITH AN OLD-SCHOOL BISCUIT SUCH AS A JAMMY DODGER OR WAGON WHEEL

Dave had always roasted his own beans, but now also supplies hotels, restaurants and pubs within a 20 mile radius. 'We only supply locally and deliver everything ourselves, so we get to know all our customers really well. In fact we class them as friends.'

Tucked away under an arch on Sheep Street, Stow Town Coffee is a delightfully diminutive coffee haven, seating just nine people alongside Gerrard the coffee roaster – which takes centre stage on the ground floor.

ESTABLISHED
2017

KEY ROASTER
Stow Town Coffee

BREWING METHOD
Espresso, filter, Chemex

MACHINE
Fracino Contempo

GRINDER
Caedo E37S

OPENING HOURS
Mon-Fri 8am-12pm
(extended in summer)

WIFI

OUTDOOR seating

DISABLED ACCESS

COFFEE COURSES

BEANS AVAILABLE
INSTORE

---

www.stowtowncoffee.co.uk   T: 01451 832519

f @stowtowncoffee   @ @stowtowncoffee

MAP № 23 KINDNESS AND CO

38 Clarence Street, Cheltenham, Gloucestershire, GL50 3JS

Knowing that when you sip single estate coffee here, a street child in Ethiopia will receive a day's food and schooling, only adds to the caffeine euphoria at this stylish Cheltenham cafe. The team is out to change the world with kindness – one cup of speciality coffee at a time.

This culture of kindness also extends to the planet: the lovely baristas use sustainably wood-roasted beans from local roaster UE, and stock Huskup coffee cups fashioned out of rice.

'We've all got used to taking a bag with us when we go shopping. Now we want to see everyone turn up for a takeaway coffee with their own cup,' says founder Carol Scott.

TIP FEEL THE LOVE WITH LATTES SUCH AS DIRTY CHAI, TURMERIC AND BEETROOT

The food menus also have kindness at their core – customers' health gets as much attention as the carefully sourced nourishing ingredients. Pea pancakes with feta, poached eggs and dukkah garner new fans daily and there are tons of temptations for veggies and vegans.

ESTABLISHED
2017

KEY ROASTER
UE Coffee
Roasters

BREWING METHOD
Espresso,
AeroPress

MACHINE
La Marzocco
Linea PB

GRINDER
Mazzer Major

OPENING HOURS
Mon-Sat **9**am-**5**pm
Sun **10**am-**4**pm

 Gluten FREE

 WIFI

 CYCLE FRIENDLY

 OUTDOOR SEATING

 FAMILY FRIENDLY

 BRING YOUR OWN CUP

---

www.kindness-and-co.com   T: 01242 6972110

f @kindnessandcocafe   🐦 @kindness_and_co   📷 @kindness_and_co

LOVE WHAT YOU DO

Olam
Specialty
Coffee

New Name. Same Places. More great coffee.

Nº24 THE COFFEE DISPENSARY

18 Regent Street, Cheltenham, Gloucestershire, GL50 1HE

Local coffee fiends have flocked to this Scandi-cool coffee shop in the centre of Cheltenham since it rocked up on Regent Street in 2015.

Showcasing a serious selection of regional roasters (think Colonna, Clifton and Round Hill) and stocking an armoury of brewing gear, The Dispensary quickly became a haunt for coffee fans of a curious disposition.

Owner Gary Marshall doesn't only stick with what's local either, so there's often also something exciting from a range of European roasters waiting to be pulled through the snazzy Sanremo Opera.

TIP MAXED OUT? TRY THE HOT CHOCOLATE SOURCED FROM WEST COAST COCOA IN NEW ZEALAND

If you're lucky enough to guinea pig a new guest, whatever's in the hopper is usually available to buy as whole beans to take away. Keen home brewers can also polish their palate at the regular cupping sessions.

While the focus is on caffeine, home-baked confections from Hetty's Kitchen and a small selection of sandwiches and panini are also available on the bar, while non-bean-based entertainment includes occasional live music nights.

ESTABLISHED
2015

KEY ROASTER
Extract Coffee Roasters

BREWING METHOD
Espresso, V60, cold brew, batch brew, AeroPress, Chemex, syphon

MACHINE
Sanremo Opera

GRINDER
Mahlkonig EK43, Mahlkonig K30

OPENING HOURS
Mon-Sat 8.30am-5.30pm
Sun 10am-4.30pm

 Gluten FREE

 BEANS AVAILABLE INSTORE

 WIFI

 CYCLE FRIENDLY

 OUTDOOR seating

 FAMILY FRIENDLY

 BRING YOUR OWN Cup

 COFFEE COURSES

www.the-coffee-dispensary.co.uk   T: 01242 260597

f @thecoffeedispensary15   🐦 @coffeedispenser   📷 @the_coffee_dispensary

MAP № 25 STAR ANISE CAFE

1 Gloucester Street, Stroud, Gloucestershire, GL5 1QG

At the core of everything at Star Anise is a wholesome and thoughtful philosophy. And if the Stroud community coffee shop's positive vibe is anything to go by, it's something we could all do with a bit more of.

Excellent coffee beans – ethically sourced and expertly roasted – travel the short hop from Extract in Bristol, before the skilled baristas take care of grinding and brewing duties. Reflecting Star Anise's focus on waste reduction, disposable cups are a no-no, so take a KeepCup if you're picking up a brew to-go.

TIP TRY THE FLAKY VEGAN CROISSANTS MADE WITH COCONUT OIL 'BUTTER' CHURNED ON-SITE DAILY

Hanging around? Settle in a cosy spot and tuck into a rainbow of (mainly) veggie and vegan dishes. Prepared according to macrobiotic principles, the food celebrates locally sourced organic produce. A commitment to developing delicious and inspiring recipes and making everything from scratch demonstrates this isn't just about paying lip service.

Community is at the heart of Star Anise, so it regularly hosts events including live music, storytelling and art exhibitions. You can even develop your skills at a sourdough-making workshop.

ESTABLISHED
2004

KEY ROASTER
Extract Coffee Roasters

BREWING METHOD
Espresso

MACHINE
Sanremo

GRINDER
Sanremo, Mythos One Clima Pro

OPENING HOURS
Mon-Fri **8.30**am-**5**pm
Sat **8.30**am-**4**pm
Sun **10**am-**2**pm

Gluten FREE

WIFI

CYCLE FRIENDLY

OUTDOOR seating

FAMILY friendly

DISABLED ACCESS

BRING YOUR OWN Cup

---

www.staraniseartscafe.com T: 01453 840021

 @staranisestroud @staranisecafe @staranisecafe

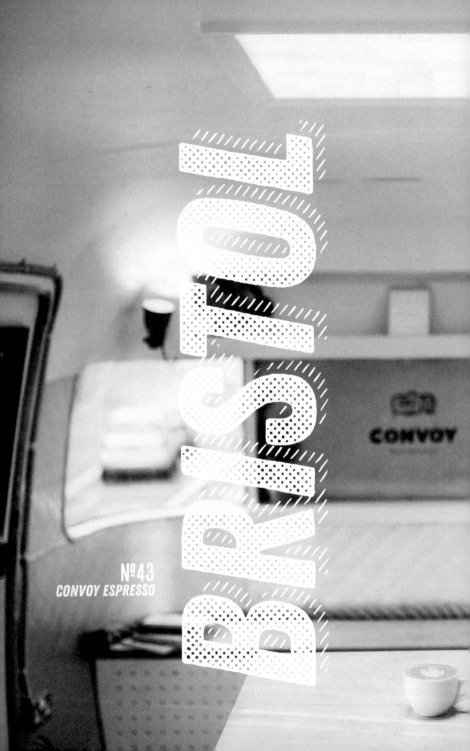

BRISTOL

№43
CONVOY ESPRESSO

CAFE

26 FED 303
27 Boston Tea Party – Gloucester Road
28 Tincan Coffee Co. – Gloucester Road
29 Tradewind Espresso
30 Coffee + Beer
31 Bakesmiths
32 Brew Coffee Company
33 The Epiphany @ RWA
34 Small Street Espresso
35 Playground Coffee and Bar
36 Spicer+Cole
37 Society Cafe – Harbourside
38 Little Victories
39 Mokoko Coffee – Wapping Wharf
40 Tincan Coffee Co. – North Street
41 Tincan Coffee Co. Trucks
42 FUELD.
43 Convoy Espresso

ROASTER

44 Extract Coffee Roasters

*All locations are approximate

MAP № 26 FED 303

303 Gloucester Road, Horfield, Bristol, BS7 8PE

This Gloucester Road newbie may be a fresher on the Bristol speciality scene, but Ross Rawling and Charlotte Hawes' new project is attracting coffee fans from across the city.

They've taken over a former butcher's shop and given the diminutive space a bright, modern makeover, adding a healthy collection of houseplants and a floor-to-ceiling menu of coffee and food crowd-pleasers.

With previous roles at pioneering companies such as Boston Tea Party and Gylly Beach Cafe, the duo know their onions. They source produce for the breakfast, lunch and cake offering from Bristol indies, while the coffee is roasted in Cornwall by Yallah.

INSIDER'S TIP
DON'T EVEN THINK ABOUT LEAVING BEFORE YOU TRY THE SALTED CHOCOLATE BROWNIES

Pair the espresso blend with milk in a flat white and lose yourself in luscious notes of chocolate, walnut and muscovado sugar.

On the foodie front, visitors will find themselves well-Fed (sorry) by vibrant salad-filled flatbreads and homebaked cakes.

ESTABLISHED
2018

KEY ROASTER
Yallah Coffee

BREWING METHOD
Espresso, filter

MACHINE
La Marzocco Linea PB

GRINDER
Compak OD

OPENING HOURS
Mon-Sat 8am-5pm
Sun 9am-5pm

---

www.fedcafe.co.uk   T: 01179 232697

f @fed303   🐦 @303fed   📷 @fed.303

MAP 27 BOSTON TEA PARTY – GLOUCESTER ROAD

293 Gloucester Road, Bristol, BS7 8PE

Boston Tea Party's Bristol branches are living up to the city's green rep this year as a result of the coffee company's blanket ban on takeaway cups.

Locals have got onboard with Boston's ballsy move to put an end to landfill-destined disposables and are embracing the changes at the busy Gloucester Road outpost.

As a former Conservative Club the building reveals quirky clues about its past – there aren't many coffee shops rocking a skittle alley floor.

TIP TAKE LITTLE ONES FOR THE AFTER-SCHOOL ACTIVITY SESSIONS

Find a nook and take time over an expertly prepared Extract filter while you contemplate the ethically-friendly brunch choices. Lemon and ricotta pancakes dripping with maple butter and topped with fresh yogurt and blueberry compote are a good call.

Veggies and vegans are also well catered for via a colourful selection of dishes that nourish from brekkie to late lunch.

ESTABLISHED
2013

KEY ROASTER
Extract Coffee Roasters

BREWING METHOD
Espresso, filter

MACHINE
La Marzocco Linea Classic

GRINDER
Mythos One Clima Pro, Mazzer Major

OPENING HOURS
Mon-Sat 7am-7pm
Sun 8am-7pm

 Gluten FREE

 BEANS AVAILABLE INSTORE

 WIFI

 CYCLE FRIENDLY

 OUTDOOR seating

 FAMILY FRIENDLY

 DISABLED ACCESS

 BRING YOUR OWN Cup

---

www.bostonteaparty.co.uk   T: 01179 241110

f @btpcafes   🐦 @btpcafes   📷 @btpcafes

MAP № 28 TINCAN COFFEE CO. – GLOUCESTER ROAD

157 Gloucester Road, Bishopston, Bristol, BS7 8BA

look out for this stylish new indie which has, fittingly, found a home in the longest row of independents in Europe and on one of the few remaining authentic high streets left in the UK.

The latest offering from the Tincan tribe (always on the lookout for ethically produced ingredients) is taking advantage of its Gloucester Road setting by sourcing from its neighbours, including buying free-range bacon and sausages from the butcher next door.

It only opened at the end of April 2018 but the cafe has already carved its niche in this fiercely independent community and become a firm favourite for a relaxed rendezvous.

TIP THE TINCAN TRUCKS ROCK UP AT FESTIVAL FIELDS ACROSS THE UK

Despite being at the helm of a growing business, owners Adam White and Jessie Nicolson are determined to stand firm when it comes to their values. The duo serve ethically sourced Clifton beans as espresso and batch brew and only use environmentally-friendly ingredients in their award winning menu of homemade sourdough toasties, cakes and pastries.

ESTABLISHED
2018

KEY ROASTER
Clifton Coffee
Roasters

BREWING METHOD
Espresso,
batch filter

MACHINE
La Marzocco
Linea PB

GRINDER
Mythos One,
Compak

OPENING HOURS
Mon-Sat 8am-6pm
Sun 9am-5pm

www.tincancoffee.co.uk   T: 01179 232076

f @tincancoffeeco   🐦 @tincancoffeeco   📷 @tincancoffeeco

MAP № 29 TRADEWIND ESPRESSO

118 Whiteladies Road, Bristol, BS8 2RP

'**P**assion and knack' is the bold assertion on the logo of the micro roaster which fuels this Bristol fave. Roasted Rituals' mantra perfectly aligns with the ethos of everyone at Tradewind – from the chefs who craft the healthy all-day brunch menu to the baristas who prepare V60s and pull espresso through the La Marzocco.

INSIDER'S TIP RAINBOW-HUED BUDDHA BOWLS CAN BE TAILORED FOR GLUTEN, DAIRY AND MEAT DODGERS

The creative bunch aim to make the coffee experience exceptional and offer an enticing range of drinks, from cold brew in summer (made with the Highground house coffee), to the must-have Biggie Smalls (a flat white served with an espresso on the side so you can taste the coffee with and without milk). A carousel of single origin beans is switched up monthly so there's always something to please a jaded palate.

The wholesome food is all made on-site, while a counter of freshly baked cakes is guaranteed to break any resolve after a single sniff.

ESTABLISHED
2012

KEY ROASTER
Roasted Rituals Coffee

BREWING METHOD
Espresso, french press, V60

MACHINE
La Marzocco Linea PB

GRINDER
Mazzer Robur Electronic

OPENING HOURS
Mon-Fri 8am-5pm
Sat 9am-5pm
Sun 9am-4pm

www.tradewindespresso.com T: 01179 743477
f @tradewindespresso118 @tradewind118 @tradewindespresso

GREAT TASTE PRODUCER

CAKESMITHS — SOUR CHERRY & HAZELNUT

CAKESMITHS — CHOCOLATE & CARAMELISED ORANGE

CAKESMITHS
CAKES FOR COFFEE SHOPS

   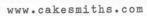 www.cakesmiths.com

cakesmithsHQ #Cakesmiths.HQ @CakesmithsHQ

EST 2014
BAKED IN BRISTOL

ᴹᵃᵖ №30 COFFEE + BEER

16 Cotham Hill, Bristol, BS6 6LF

It's a fairly safe bet that the kind of people who care where their coffee comes from follow the same philosophy regarding beer. And with this in mind, Dan Williams decided to cover all the beverage bases when he opened his aptly named Coffee + Beer in 2017.

Caffeine-based kicks at the Cotham Hill hangout are sourced from a selection of South West roasters – Origin, Round Hill, Extract – with guest spots for less-local roasteries such as Square Mile.

TIP TRY BEFORE YOU BUY WITH A SELECTION OF SIX 'LOOSE' COFFEES

Don't be daunted by the chunky choice of bean providers as Dan's always up for sharing his pick of the latest crop: *'I really enjoy introducing newcomers to speciality and sending them off on their coffee journey.'*

With a new on-site alcohol licence, you can enjoy a draught craft beer from the selection of six taps – as well as a cracking curation of coffee cocktails – while you contemplate which of the bottled line-up you'll pick up for later.

Need some sustenance before cracking into the bevvies? Find a small selection of Bristol-baked pastries and cakes on the counter.

ESTABLISHED
2017

KEY ROASTER
Multiple roasters

BREWING METHOD
Espresso, drip filter, Kalita Wave

MACHINE
La Marzocco GS3

GRINDER
Mythos One Clima Pro, Mahlkonig EK43

OPENING HOURS
Mon-Wed 8am-5pm
Thu 8am-7pm
Fri 8am-9pm
Sat 10am-9pm

Gluten FREE

BEANS AVAILABLE INSTORE

WIFI

CYCLE FRIENDLY

FAMILY FRIENDLY

DISABLED ACCESS

BRING YOUR OWN Cup

www.coffeeandbeer.co.uk   T: 01173 293010

f @coffeeandbeerbristol 🐦 @coffeeandbeeruk 📷 @coffeeandbeer_bristol

MAP № 31 BAKESMITHS

65 Whiteladies Road, Bristol, BS8 2LY

Intrepid coffee folk touring the region's caffeine capital know to schedule a lunchtime stop at this corner coffee shop. And it's not just to scoff Bakesmiths' dirty beans and smoked salmon brunch plates – it's to take advantage of the opportunity to stuff their canvas totes with as many of the house bakes as they can haul home.

If you're a seasoned speciality fan you've probably already sampled a few of the bejewelled traybakes and epic brownies which crowd Bakesmiths' counter – just not necessarily here. That's because sister company Cakesmiths stocks top-notch cafes across the country with its Bristol-baked beauties.

TIP DON'T LEAVE WITHOUT PICKING UP A LOAF OF STEVE'S SERIOUSLY GOOD SOURDOUGH

Maple and pecan smothered sticky buns; kale, hummus and herb stuffed twists; and fat slices of Seville orange and chocolate traycake served at the Whiteladies Road cafe are complemented by a sterling roast (care of Clifton Coffee).

The Bristol roaster crafts an espresso and filter blend especially for the cafe which, when served with milk, yields notes of cocoa and caramel.

ESTABLISHED
2016

KEY ROASTER
Clifton Coffee
Roasters

BREWING METHOD
Espresso,
filter

MACHINE
La Marzocco
Linea

GRINDER
Compak E8

OPENING HOURS
Mon-Fri 8am-5pm
Sat 9am-5pm
Sun 10am-4pm

Gluten FREE

BEANS AVAILABLE
INSTORE

WIFI

OUTDOOR seating

FAMILY FRIENDLY

BRING YOUR OWN Cup

---

www.bakesmiths.co.uk   T: 07535 607061

f @bakesmithshq   🐦 @bakesmithshq   📷 @bakesmiths_hq

MAP№ 32 BREW COFFEE COMPANY

45 Whiteladies Road, Clifton, Bristol, BS8 2LS

A nomadic mix of antipodean adventure and vibrant Middle Eastern flavours come together to create a brunch bill worth travelling for at Bristol's Brew Coffee Company.

Whether you go long haul via colourful compilations such as the poached eggs with bacon, labneh, pomegranate and mint or stay closer to home with the Brew beans on toast, the accompanying flattie or filter coffee is roasted in the city by the beansmiths at Clifton.

Along with a menu refresh, Brew's band of super-smiley baristas were excited to have a spin on the snazzy Marco SP9 batch brewer when it arrived earlier this year. Give 'em a chance to show off the new kit and order the guest single origin coffee as filter for a fruity hit.

TIP HEAD TO THE SPACIOUS DECKING FOR SUNSHINE-SPLASHED SIPPING

Handcrafted gifts and homewares from local indies such as Handmade by Vix and Elizabeth James give visitors plenty to feast their eyes on before they dig into a plate of Turkish eggs with homemade harissa, labneh and roasted kale.

ESTABLISHED
2014

KEY ROASTER
Clifton Coffee Roasters

BREWING METHOD
Espresso, pourover

MACHINE
La Marzocco Linea PB

GRINDER
Nuova Simonelli

OPENING HOURS
Mon-Fri 7.30am-6pm
Sat 8am-6pm
Sun 9am-5pm

 Gluten FREE

 BEANS AVAILABLE INSTORE

 WIFI

 CYCLE FRIENDLY

 OUTDOOR SEATING

 FAMILY FRIENDLY

 DISABLED ACCESS

 BRING YOUR OWN CUP

www.brewcoffeecompany.co.uk   T: 01179 732842

f @brewcoffeecompany   🐦 @brewcc   📷 @brewcc

MAP 33 THE EPIPHANY @ RWA

Royal West of England Academy, Queens Road, Clifton, Bristol, BS8 1PX

Carefully crafted flat whites and beautiful brunch plates are perfectly placed in the Royal West of England Academy gallery's picturesque cafe.

A fuchsia neon sign above the bar and the scent of fresh-from-the-oven fancies (co-owner Beth bakes wicked passionfruit pasteis de nata and cracking sausage rolls) lure passing arty-types into the contemporary coffee shop.

INSIDER'S TIP GORGEOUS DAY? THE SUN TRAP BALCONY OVERLOOKS THE WHOLE OF CLIFTON TRIANGLE

But while the kitchen's creative concoctions persuade newbies to peruse the menu, it's the coffee which keeps the caffeine purists coming back. Bristol's Extract stump up the good stuff for the grinder and there are regular guest spots from the likes of Girls Who Grind and Koppi.

Supporting coffee farmers is important to co-owner and UK Barista Championship finalist Alex, which is why he travelled to Peru with Extract last year to visit the farmers who grow The Epiphany's house espresso.

And look out for The Epiphany coffee van which will soon be rocking up at local festivals, markets and events.

ESTABLISHED
2017

KEY ROASTER
Extract Coffee Roasters

BREWING METHOD
Espresso, batch brew, V60, Clever Dripper

MACHINE
La Marzocco Linea Classic

GRINDER
Mythos One Clima Pro

OPENING HOURS
Tue-Thu 9am-5pm
Fri 9am-4.30pm
Sat 10am-5PM
Sun 11am-4.30pm

Gluten FREE

BEANS AVAILABLE / INSTORE

WIFI

CYCLE FRIENDLY

OUTDOOR seating

FAMILY FRIENDLY

DISABLED ACCESS

BRING YOUR OWN CUP

---

www.theepiphanyrwa.com   T: 01173 179816

f @theepiphanyrwa   @theepiphanyrwa

MAP: 34 SMALL STREET ESPRESSO

23 Small Street, Bristol, BS1 1DW

Small Street has been a key player on the Bristol coffee scene since 2012 and its recent Best Coffee Shop win at the Bristol Good Food Awards 2018 further cements its status as one of the city's best loved speciality spots.

Office folk, caffeine tourists and students all seek solace at Small Street, piling in to the petite space for a fix of the Clifton Coffee house blend. Those with time to spare are advised to secure a corner seat and linger over the tasting notes as they sip the latest guest from a line-up of South West roasters.

INSIDER'S TIP ON SUNNY DAYS, PERCH ON THE BENCH OUT FRONT AND CHILL WITH A COLD BREW AND TONIC

Nearby St Nicholas Market caters to cavernous appetites, though Small Street's short 'n' sweet selection of sourdough sarnies and counter of carby faves are enough to gratify the greed of most. A slice of buttery toasted banana bread and a glossy flat white come highly recommended as a killer start to the day.

ESTABLISHED
2012

KEY ROASTER
Clifton Coffee Roasters

BREWING METHOD
Espresso, V60, cold brew

MACHINE
La Marzocco FB80

GRINDER
Mythos One Clima Pro, Mahlkonig EK43

OPENING HOURS
Mon-Fri **7.30**am-**4.30**pm
Sat **9.30**am-**4.30**pm

www.smallstreetespresso.co.uk

f @smallstespresso 🐦 @smallstespresso 📷 @smallstespresso

MAP № 35 PLAYGROUND COFFEE AND BAR

45 St Nicholas Street, Bristol, BS1 1TP

Don't get too attached to the single origin you're sipping at this convivial coffee shop as owners Fabian and Lilly rarely feature a coffee twice.

Playground's snug space on St Nicholas Street may feature a swing in the window and more board games than you can shake a KerPlunk stick at, but this place is super serious when it comes to the caffeine which fuels the fun. Guest roasts change on a weekly basis, the house coffee comes from experts at Colonna and blends are a big no-no.

This doesn't mean that the team don't like to let loose though. Blending quality caffeine with artisan spirits is the ultimate pastime at Playground and coffee cocktails such as the Dark and Stormy – rum, cold brew, ginger beer and lime – are served (until late) from Thursday to Saturday.

INSIDER'S TIP — HIRE THE UNIQUE SPACE FOR A COFFEE SHOP SHINDIG

The crew aren't shabby when it comes to shaking up an espresso martini either – team Playground came second at the European Coffee Mixology Championships at the Amsterdam Coffee Festival.

ESTABLISHED
2014

KEY ROASTER
Colonna Coffee

BREWING METHOD
Espresso, V60

MACHINE
La Marzocco Linea

GRINDER
Mahlkonig K30 Twin, Mahlkonig K30 Vario

OPENING HOURS
Mon-Wed 10am-5pm
Thu-Fri 10am-11pm
Sat 10.30am-11pm
Sun 11.30am-4.30pm

 Gluten FREE

 BEANS AVAILABLE / INSTORE

 WIFI

 CYCLE FRIENDLY

 OUTDOOR seating

 DISABLED ACCESS

 BRING YOUR OWN cup

COFFEE COURSES

---

www.playgroundcoffee.co.uk

 f @playgroundcoffeehouse   🐦 @playgroundcofco   📷 @playgroundcoffeehouse

^{MAP} 36 SPICER+COLE

1 Queen Square Avenue, Bristol, BS1 4JA

In a light-filled space just a whisker from Bristol's achingly cool waterfront, Spicer+Cole have nailed the pretty-damn-near-perfect coffee and food combo.

For the house blend, visitors are whizzed to Colombia, Peru and El Salvador, by way of Extract, which roasts a mere bean's skim across the city. An array of guests that include Crankhouse, Girls Who Grind and Climpson, get their turn on rotation and ensure there's never a dull moment.

TIP GRAB A BRANDED KEEPCUP AND DO THE ENVIRONMENT (AND YOUR BANK ACCOUNT) A FAVOUR

With baristas benefitting from Extract's expert training, every cup squeezed from the La Marzocco Linea is a work of balanced excellence. And when the sun comes out, so does Spicer+Cole's homemade cold brew.

Accompaniments to your coffee are almost overwhelmingly tempting. The piled-high food counter (inspired by glorious continental markets) is a kaleidoscope of salads, tarts and frittata, all homemade using locally sourced, seasonal and sustainable ingredients. Take care not to fill up – you'll want a slice of courgette and lime cake to follow, trust us.

ESTABLISHED
2012

KEY ROASTER
Extract Coffee Roasters

BREWING METHOD
Espresso, cold brew

MACHINE
La Marzocco Linea PB

GRINDER
Mythos

OPENING HOURS
Mon-Fri 7.30am-5pm
Sat 8.30am-5pm
Sun 9am-4pm

www.spicerandcole.co.uk   T: 01179 220513
f @spicerandcole @spicerandcole @spicerandcole

· 2018 ·

SOUTH WEST HIGHLIGHTS

EXTRACT COFFEE ROASTERS

ROASTING FOR THE LOCALS

SUPPORTING 17 CHARITIES
ACROSS THE SOUTH WEST

SCA
Competition Finalists

!!

24/7

TECHNICAL
SUPPORT
ACROSS THE
SOUTH WEST

FREE BARISTA TRAINING

OVER 1000

TRAINED
A YEAR

SHARING KNOWLEDGE
AT COFFEE HOUSE
PROJECT

EXTRACTCOFFEE.CO.UK

37 SOCIETY CAFE – HARBOURSIDE

Farrs Lane, Narrow Quay, Bristol, BS1 4BD

Society's biggest outpost is the baby of the four-strong bunch and has just celebrated 365 days of fabulous flat whites and Bristol Harbour views.

Sitting on the newly pedestrianised harbourside, the spacious coffee shop is an oasis of calm in the city and a coveted spot in which to relax and appreciate the craft of exceptional caffeine.

Beans to be explored from one of the cafe's cosy corners (or on the splatter of alfresco furniture) hail from Cornwall, where Origin carefully roast the best of the season's crop. The Society team work closely with the artisan roaster and recently joined them on a coffee trip to Nicaragua.

TIP INTO PHOTOGRAPHY? DROP YOUR FILMS OFF AT THE CAFE TO BE DEVELOPED

A who's who of speciality roasters join Origin on the brew bar – Bailies, Crankhouse and Round Hill to name a few – so it's worth asking the barista what's new and tasting terrific. If you've time to linger over your filter, there's a collection of beautiful photography books and magazines to flick through as well as regularly updated exhibitions.

ESTABLISHED
2017

KEY ROASTER
Origin Coffee Roasters

BREWING METHOD
Espresso, batch brew, AeroPress, cold brew

MACHINE
La Marzocco Linea PB

GRINDER
Mythos One, Mahlkonig EK43

OPENING HOURS
Mon-Sat 7.30am-6.30pm
Sun 9am-6pm

www.society-cafe.com   T: 01179 304660

f @societycafebath   @societycafe   @societycafe

MAP 38 LITTLE VICTORIES

7 Gaol Ferry Steps, Wapping Wharf, Bristol, BS1 6WE

This sister shop to Small Street Espresso is likely to earn a spot on your revisit list thanks to its harbourside location, easy-going atmosphere and killer coffee offering.

It's a good job too as it will take at least three trips to make a dent on the 10ft letterpress menu.

We'd recommend starting with beans, roasted by Bristol stalwart Clifton Coffee, before moving on to the bill of natural wines and craft beers.

TIP GRAB ONE OF THE WINDOW STOOLS AND IMMERSE YOURSELF IN THE WORLD OF WAPPING WHARF

Ask the barista which of the board's espresso and filter options are best that day – there are usually two of each – and then get cracking on the coffee-inspired cocktails (note: the cold brew negroni is knockout).

A simple selection of pastries, sourdough and sandwiches fuels daytime visitors, while evening drinks are imbibed over boards of local cheese and Spanish olives. After-dark events are a regular occurrence and feature everything from live music to cake and beer pairings.

ESTABLISHED
2016

KEY ROASTER
Clifton Coffee Roasters

BREWING METHOD
Espresso, Chemex, cold brew

MACHINE
Victoria Arduino Black Eagle

GRINDER
Mythos One Clima Pro, Mahlkonig EK43

OPENING HOURS
Mon **7.30**am-**5**pm
Tue-Wed **7.30**am-**7**pm
Thu-Fri **7.30**am-**10**pm
Sat **9**am-**10**pm
Sun **9**am-**5**pm

www.littlevics.co.uk
f @littlevicsbristol @littlevicsbris @littlevicsbris

MAP № 39 MOKOKO COFFEE – WAPPING WHARF

2 Gaol Ferry Steps, Wapping Wharf, Bristol, BS1 6WE

Mokoko's Bristol outpost and bakery HQ has had a pretty impressive year – it not only scooped a Taste of the West Gold award but also bagged three Great Taste Awards for its line-up of lovely loaf cakes, fruit-laden tarts and gravity-defying cruffins (the croissant-muffin love child).

If collecting accolades hasn't kept the creative team busy enough, taking the coffee sourcing operation in-house and stocking its three coffee shops with a selection of single origin beans certainly increased Mokoko's 2018 to-do list.

TIP GRAB A SEAT ON THE LOWER LEVEL AND WATCH THE BAKERS CRAFT THE NEXT BATCH OF CRUFFINS

The trio of Mokoko cafes – including the Wapping Wharf outpost – receive a hot-from-the-roaster supply of seasonal beans from HQ. South American, Central American and African roasts all feature and are available to buy as whole beans from the venues, as well as from the Mokoko website.

Local roasteries Extract and James Gourmet give the gang a well-earned rest and take turns in the guest grinder. Try something fruity on filter and pair it with a slab of the award winning beetroot and ginger cake.

ESTABLISHED
2016

KEY ROASTER
Mokoko

BREWING METHOD
Espresso, Kalita Wave, drip, AeroPress, batch brew

MACHINE
Conti Monte Carlo

GRINDER
Compak E10 Master

OPENING HOURS
Mon-Fri 7.30am-5.30pm
Sat 8am-6.30pm
Sun 9am-6.30pm

Gluten FREE · BEANS AVAILABLE INSTORE · WIFI · CYCLE FRIENDLY · OUTDOOR SEATING · DISABLED ACCESS · BRING YOUR OWN CUP

www.mokokocoffee.com T: 01179 290177
f @mokokocoffee @mokokocoffee @mokokocoffee

MAP Nº 40 TINCAN COFFEE CO. – NORTH STREET

234 North Street, Southville, Bristol, BS3 1JD

After rescuing a rusty old campervan from almost certain atrophy in a French field, Adam White and Jessie Nicolson began building their fleet of lovingly restored vintage coffee trucks from which they plied festival goers with great coffee.

Nowadays you can also sip Tincan coffee at a couple of bricks and mortar outlets, but the cafes still reference their iconic vans: look out for headlamp lighting and booth seating based on truck seats.

TIP INSIDER'S
AVO IS OFF THE MENU AT THIS ECO-FRIENDLY JOINT DUE TO ENVIRONMENTAL CONCERNS

This Southville gaff serves the house seasonal espresso blend, roasted by Clifton, and also offers bean buffs the opportunity to experiment with new flavours via a rolling line-up of guest espressos and single origin filters.

Tincan's Best Cafe Food 2018 win at the Bristol Good Food Awards makes total sense when you check out the seasonally changing brunch menu (with plenty of options for those abstaining from sugar, gluten, meat or animal products) and fresh-from-the-oven delights such as banana and peanut butter muffins.

ESTABLISHED
2016

KEY ROASTER
Clifton Coffee Roasters

BREWING METHOD
Espresso, batch filter

MACHINE
La Marzocco Linea PB

GRINDER
Mythos One, Compak

OPENING HOURS
Mon-Sat 8am-6pm
Sun 9am-5pm

 Gluten FREE

 BEANS AVAILABLE INSTORE

 WIFI

 CYCLE FRIENDLY

 OUTDOOR seating

 FAMILY FRIENDLY

 BRING YOUR OWN cup

---

www.tincancoffee.co.uk   T: 01179 633979

f @tincancoffeeco   🐦 @tincancoffeeco   📷 @tincancoffeeco

MAP № 41 TINCAN COFFEE CO. TRUCKS

Music festivals and high profile sporting events around the UK

Outstanding in the field? You wouldn't expect any less from this cool collection of 1960s and 70s vintage trucks which have been seeing off the competition and serving top-notch coffee in meadows across the country since 2011.

When hanging about in the rain after a terrible night's sleep on a camping mat, most festival goers don't relish the idea of a vapid and tepid brew served from the back of a burger van. But these days they don't need to as, by rocking up at one of Tincan's beautifully restored coffee trucks (named Claude, Wilfred, Dennis, Woody, Napolean and Alfie), they can be assured of an expertly prepared speciality-grade espresso, crafted from Bristol-roasted Clifton beans.

TIP BRISTOLIANS CAN GET THEIR TINCAN FIX ON GLOUCESTER ROAD AND NORTH STREET

Whether they've been at Blue Dot, Festival No6, Shambala or Queen's, music and sport fans haven't had to forgo warming their fingers on a decent cup of coffee this year – or, for that matter, enjoying iced blends and award winning cakes to accompany their entertainment of choice.

ESTABLISHED
2011

KEY ROASTER
Clifton Coffee Roasters

BREWING METHOD
Espresso

MACHINE
La Spaziale S5

GRINDER
Mazzer

OPENING HOURS
As per event

www.tincancoffee.co.uk   T: 07725 880581

f @tincancoffeeco   🐦 @tincancoffeeco   📷 @tincancoffeeco

MAP № 42 FUELD.

Unit 1, 2 Glass Wharf, Bristol, BS2 0EL

Visitors to this Glass Wharf newcomer can tick 'workout' and 'coffee' off their to-do list in one go as the swanky set-up adjoins Starks Fitness. So if you're feeling energetic, you can grab a turmeric latte and tone your lats, all under one roof.

Desk-bound office workers have already made this glass-panelled oasis their go-to for healthy grub (the fridge heaves with freshly rustled up takeaway breakfast and lunch options). The other draw is the expertly crafted coffee made with beans roasted by Clifton – choose from V60, espresso, batch and cold brew.

INSIDERS TIP: TRY A CLIFTON LIFT: A DOUBLE ESPRESSO AND ALMOND MILKSHAKE

FUELD. wears its healthy credentials with pride: a dazzling array of juices are made on-site every morning, including Nadia's Glow (beetroot, apple, basil and lemon) and Slim Greens (kale, cucumber, celery and apple). Grab a stool at one of the funky yellow tables and tuck into superfood compilations such as the famous protein pancakes (gluten-free oats, egg, banana, cinnamon, almond butter, blueberry and protein powder) or a healthy Hawaiian poke bowl.

ESTABLISHED
2018

KEY ROASTER
Clifton Coffee Roasters

BREWING METHOD
Espresso, V60, batch brew, cold brew

MACHINE
Victoria Arduino Black Eagle

GRINDER
Victoria Arduino Mythos One, Mahlkonig EK43

OPENING HOURS
Mon-Fri **6**am-**9**pm
Sat-Sun **8**am-**2**pm

Gluten FREE

 WiFi

 CYCLE FRIENDLY

 OUTDOOR seating

---

www.fueld.co.uk   T: 01173 258169

@wearefueld

№43 CONVOY ESPRESSO

Paintworks, Bath Road, Bristol, BS4 3EH

It's a well-known fact that creativity can't exist without caffeine. Which is why the absence of decent coffee at Paintworks, Bristol's creative hub, bemused chums Colin, Josh and Zak.

Rather than just grumbling, however, the guys took the initiative and brought coffee to the people via two gleaming Airstreams. Now co-workers, creatives and coffee folk can sip in Scandi-minimalist surrounds, or enjoy a cup outdoors, while soaking up the artsy vibes.

INSIDER'S TIP NO-FUSS ACCESS AND BIKE RACKS MEAN CAFFEINE-FUELLED CYCLISTS CAN EASILY GRAB A BREW

The house roast is refreshed every few months and makes its way to Bristol via Origin's Cornish roastery. There's also a regular guest roast from local favourites such as Bristol's Triple Co Roast, and pourovers to showcase the latest clean and complex flavour profiles.

A frequently refreshed menu offers pastries and Convoy's speciality: sourdough toasties. And to start the day, avo on toast and vegan energy balls are a winner. Need more to get the creative juices flowing? The gang also serve freshly blitzed smoothies and craft beer.

ESTABLISHED
2018

KEY ROASTER
Origin Coffee Roasters

BREWING METHOD
Espresso, Chemex, Kalita Wave, batch brew

MACHINE
La Marzocco Linea PB

GRINDER
Mythos One Clima Pro, Mahlkonig EK43

OPENING HOURS
Mon-Fri 7.30am-3.30pm

  WIFI

 CYCLE FRIENDLY

 OUTDOOR seating

 BRING YOUR OWN Cup

www.convoyespresso.com   T: 07754 299087

f @convoyespresso   @ @convoyespresso

BRISTOL
ROASTERS

MAP 44 EXTRACT COFFEE ROASTERS

Unit 1, Gatton Road, Bristol, BS2 9SH

2018 saw Extract further demonstrate its commitment to building win-win relationships with farmers while delivering crowd-pleasing, single origin coffees for their loyal fans.

In sourcing the best beans the net is cast far and wide, taking in Ethiopia, Guatemala and Colombia where farmers struggle with market and climate challenges. These beans make up the brand's hero-range such as Cast Iron or go into limited editions including Unkle Funka and Strong Man.

Community is close to the growing team's heart and their roastery doors often open for tastings, events or just a quick brew. The wider coffee world also beats a path to the roastery to take advantage of the barista training and SCA courses.

'CALLUM AND JAMES REPRESENTED EXTRACT IN THE UKBC AND COFFEE IN GOOD SPIRITS FINALS'

Riding on the crest of the collaboration wave, Extract has also somehow found the energy to craft a stonking coffee IPA with Bristol neighbours Wiper & True, while Callum and James represented Extract in the UK Barista Championship and Coffee in Good Spirits finals.

ESTABLISHED
2007

ROASTER
MAKE & SIZE
Probat 120kg
Probat 60kg
Petroncini 30kg
Ozturk 4kg

OPEN
BY APPOINTMENT

OPEN
TO THE PUBLIC

COFFEE
COURSES

COURSES

BEANS
AVAILABLE

www.extractcoffee.co.uk   T: 01179 554976

f @extractcoffeeroasters   @extractcoffee   @extractcoffee

BATH & SOMER-SET

Nº46
BOSTON TEA PARTY –
KINGSMEAD SQUARE

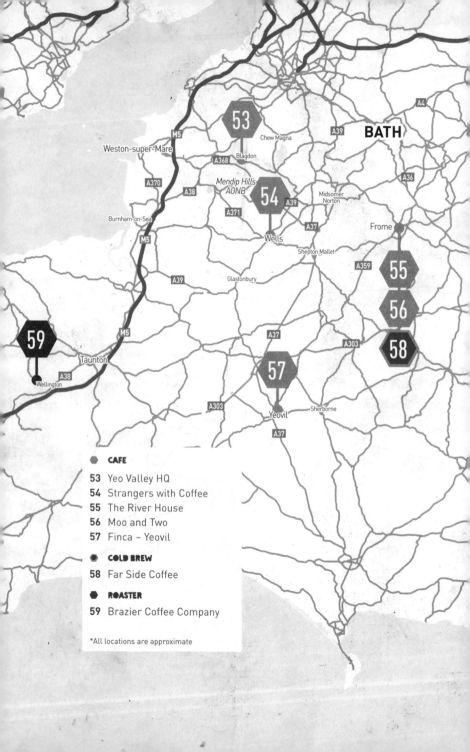

CAFE

53 Yeo Valley HQ
54 Strangers with Coffee
55 The River House
56 Moo and Two
57 Finca – Yeovil

COLD BREW

58 Far Side Coffee

ROASTER

59 Brazier Coffee Company

*All locations are approximate

● CAFE

45 Colonna & Small's
46 Boston Tea Party – Kingsmead Square
47 The Bath Coffee Company
48 Society Cafe – Kingsmead Square
49 Lulu Caffe
50 Picnic Coffee
51 Society Cafe – The Corridor
52 Mokoko Coffee – Southgate

*All locations are approximate

MAP 45 COLONNA & SMALL'S

6 Chapel Row, Bath, BA1 1HN

The pros at Colonna Coffee have continued to push the bean-sourcing boundaries this year. And this Bath coffee shop, where Colonna's journey into exceptional caffeine began, is the perfect place to explore the roastery's intriguing range of single origins.

Three time UK barista champ and South West speciality pioneer Maxwell Colonna-Dashwood and wife Lesley founded the Chapel Row cafe in 2009. This was followed by the launch of the roasting arm of the business (on the outskirts of Bristol) in 2015.

INSIDER'S TIP HANDSOME HUNKS OF CAKE MAKE GOOD COMPANY FOR THE EXQUISITELY CRAFTED BREWS

Since then, Colonna's seasonal house-roasted coffees have replaced the likes of Has Bean in the copper-coloured Mahlkonig grinder. Selecting beans is made simpler for visitors via the Foundation, Discovery and Rare coffee categories, while a brigade of highly skilled baristas are on hand to help you choose between espresso, lungo, AeroPress and syphon serves.

Coffees to take home for further exploration are available to buy and, if you're more Nespresso than pourover, speciality grade capsules are also available.

ESTABLISHED
2009

KEY ROASTER
Colonna Coffee

BREWING METHOD
Espresso, lungo, AeroPress, syphon

MACHINE
Modbar

GRINDER
Mahlkonig EK43

OPENING HOURS
Mon-Fri 8am-5.30pm
Sat 8.30am-5.30pm
Sun 10am-4pm

Gluten FREE

BEANS AVAILABLE
INSTORE

WIFI

OUTDOOR seating

BRING YOUR OWN cup

---

www.colonnaandsmalls.co.uk   T: 07766 808067

f @colonnaandsmalls   🐦 @colonna_smalls   📷 @colonnacoffee

MAP № 46 BOSTON TEA PARTY – KINGSMEAD SQUARE

19 Kingsmead Square, Bath, BA1 2AE

O ne of the first cafes in the ever-burgeoning Boston brigade, Bath's BTP is a caffeine institution in the city.

A lot has happened since the first flat whites were poured here and the West Country mini-chain is now a changemaker in the battle against plastic waste. Boston's blanket ban on single-use cups (since May 2018) has already saved tens of thousands of disposables heading to landfill, and the eco-conscious team hope that other indies will follow their lead.

INSIDER'S TIP LOVE THE EXTRACT HOUSE BLEND? PICK UP A BAG OF BEANS TO BREW AT HOME

Don't sweat, you can still pick up your Extract house blend espresso to-go, just remember to pack a takeaway cup. Forgetful regulars are covered by the cafe's cup loan scheme and collection of retail reuseables.

It's not just about being eco-warriors though, as serving top-notch coffee in vibrant locations is still priority number one, and this venue's position on Bath's buzzy Kingsmead Square fits the mould nicely.

On warm days head to the alfresco seating to brunch on pancakes while you watch the shoppers scurry by.

ESTABLISHED
2013

KEY ROASTER
Extract Coffee Roasters

BREWING METHOD
Espresso, filter

MACHINE
La Marzocco Linea PB

GRINDER
Mythos One Clima Pro, Mazzer Major

OPENING HOURS
Mon-Sat 7am-7pm
Sun 8am-7pm

Gluten FREE

BEANS AVAILABLE IN STORE

WIFI

CYCLE FRIENDLY

OUTDOOR seating

FAMILY FRIENDLY

BRING YOUR OWN Cup.

---

www.bostonteaparty.co.uk   T: 01225 314826

f @btpcafes   🐦 @btpcafes   📷 @btpcafes

MAP № 47 THE BATH COFFEE COMPANY

14 Kingsmead Square, Bath, BA1 2AD

Whatever perplexing conundrum you're currently mulling over, a good place to look for answers is in a cup of The Solution.

The Brazilian-Indian-Sumatran house blend at Bath Coffee Company's cosy cafe certainly resolves any uncertainties as to which shops to hit up next, or whether to throw in the towel and instead stay and chill for a while. In fact, after a few sips of this espresso (bronzed at the cafe's Wiltshire roastery, Square Root), the only dilemma you'll be left with is: what to try next from the drinks menu.

Grab a moment with owner Adrian Smith (he's also master roaster at Square Root) to chat through the filter options, or quiz the baristas who constantly build on their knowledge through regular cuppings and tastings.

TIP TRY AN AMERITINI (NON-ALCOHOLIC ESPRESSO MARTINI) FOR A DAYTIME BUZZ

With a friendly welcome, comfy sofas, daily-changing cakes, retro board games and coffee expertise, the cafe's award for Bath's Best Coffee 2018 from the *Bath Chronicle* tells you everything you need to know.

ESTABLISHED
2014

KEY ROASTER
Square Root Coffee

BREWING METHOD
Espresso, V60, AeroPress

MACHINE
La Pavoni

GRINDER
La Pavoni, Graef, Cunill

OPENING HOURS
Mon-Sun 8am-6pm

Gluten FREE

BEANS AVAILABLE IN-STORE

WIFI

CYCLE FRIENDLY

OUTDOOR seating

FAMILY FRIENDLY

BRING YOUR OWN cup.

---

www.bathcoffeecompany.co.uk   T: 07940 120835

f @thebathcoffeeco   @ @bathcoffeecompany

MAP № 48 SOCIETY CAFE – KINGSMEAD SQUARE

5 Kingsmead Square, Bath, BA1 2AB

It's been a busy year at Society's flagship coffee shop. The crowds of caffeine fans flocking to Kingsmead Square for a fix have been part of the reason, of course, but it's been exacerbated by a lively line-up of coffee comps, brewing courses and photography exhibitions.

While the ever-changing schedule has been non-stop for owners Adrian and Jane and their team, the specially roasted house coffee from Origin has remained consistently exceptional.

TIP DEDICATED BIKE RACKS OUTSIDE THE SHOP MAKE IT SUPER CYCLE FRIENDLY

The Cornish roaster has been joined by a carousel of guest beans, so even regulars can find something new to savour as they nestle in a nook with the latest batch brew.

Don't worry if you visit sans-paperback as you'll find plenty of entertainment in the large collection of photography books and indie mags scattered throughout the cafe. Freshly blitzed smoothies and hunks of traybake fuel the creative conversations and ideas that follow a flick through the latest issues.

ESTABLISHED
2012

KEY ROASTER
Origin Coffee Roasters

BREWING METHOD
Espresso, AeroPress cold brew, batch brew

MACHINE
La Marzocco Linea PB

GRINDER
Mahlkonig K30, Mahlkonig Tanzania, Nuova Simonelli Mythos

OPENING HOURS
Mon-Fri 7am-6.30pm
Sat 7.30am-6.30pm
Sun 9am-6pm

Gluten FREE

BEANS AVAILABLE INSTORE

WIFI

CYCLE FRIENDLY

OUTDOOR SEATING

FAMILY FRIENDLY

DISABLED ACCESS

BRING YOUR OWN CUP

www.society-cafe.com   T: 01225 442433
f @societycafebath   @societycafe   @societycafe

MAP 49 LULU CAFFE

1 Hot Bath Street, Bath, BA1 1SJ

A translation of 'pearl' in Arabic, Lulu Caffe was named *'to reflect the way in which precious coffee beans shimmer like refined pearls once extracted into a cup,'* explains owner Mohammad.

Launching the olive green cafe in a corner of Bath in 2016, Mohammad sought to blend the city's passion for speciality with his own Levant caffeine culture (more commonly known as Turkish coffee).

TIP PAIR YOUR TURKISH COFFEE WITH A SQUARE OF AUTHENTIC TURKISH DELIGHT

The result is a welcoming space where traditional pot coffee is served alongside espresso, pourover and AeroPress, brewed with beans from local roasteries Clifton and Round Hill.

'We aim to reflect the original roots of Levant culture through the aroma, texture and taste of authentic Arabic coffee,' continues Mohammad.

Take the experience to the next level with homemade dishes such as falafel and chicken shawarma.

ESTABLISHED
2016

KEY ROASTER
Clifton Coffee
Roasters

BREWING METHOD
Espresso,
Clever Dripper,
AeroPress

MACHINE
La Marzocco

GRINDER
Mahlkonig K30,
Mahlkonig K30 twin

OPENING HOURS
Mon-Sun **8**am-**6**pm

 Gluten FREE

 BEANS AVAILABLE INSTORE

 WIFI

 CYCLE FRIENDLY

 OUTDOOR seating

 FAMILY FRIENDLY

DISABLED ACCESS

 BRING YOUR OWN cup

T: 07459 432120

f @lulucaffe.bath 🐦 @lulucaffe.bath 📷 @lulucaffe.bath

MAP 50 PICNIC COFFEE

9 Saracen Street, Bath, BA1 5BR

When you need a breather from Bath's boutiques and coach-tour bustle, duck down Saracen Street into the welcoming warmth of Picnic Coffee.

They've got a continental thing going on at the popular coffee shop, with a vibe so laid back it's almost horizontal. Watch the world from a well-chosen window seat as you savour a cup brewed by infectiously cheerful staff.

TIP LOOK OUT FOR REGULAR COMMUNITY-FOCUSED EVENTS SUCH AS PLANT SALES AND ART EXHIBITIONS

Though it's informal, Picnic takes speciality super seriously. The journey of the beans from farm to roastery to your lips is emphasised and focuses on expertise at every stage. Has Bean takes star billing as roaster of choice and is ably assisted by guests from Round Hill.

Meticulously balanced espresso comes courtesy of the VA Black Eagle, or plump for V60 pourover or AeroPress. Loose-leaf teas can be mixed for a bespoke combo and come with a pre-set timer that chimes when the brew's perfect.

Treats and tickles mean doggy friends will be as keen as you to pop into Picnic.

ESTABLISHED
2013

KEY ROASTER
Has Bean Coffee

BREWING METHOD
Espresso, V60, AeroPress

MACHINE
Victoria Arduino Black Eagle

GRINDER
Victoria Arduino Mythos One, Mahlkonig EK43 S, Mahlkonig K30

OPENING HOURS
Mon-Fri **7.30**am-**6**pm
Sat **8.30**am-**6**pm
Sun **9**am-**6**pm

Gluten FREE

BEANS AVAILABLE
INSTORE

WIFI

CYCLE FRIENDLY

OUTDOOR Seating

DISABLED ACCESS

BRING YOUR OWN Cup

---

www.picniccoffee.co.uk   T: 01225 330128

f @picniccoffee   🐦 @picnic_bath   📷 @picnic_bath

ᴹᴬᴾ№ 51 SOCIETY CAFE – THE CORRIDOR

19 High Street, Bath, BA1 5AJ

This pocket-sized coffee shop on Bath's busy High Street is changing the on-the-go coffee game – one guest filter and seasonal single origin espresso at a time.

The team behind Society's small band of boutique cafes are a promiscuous bunch and have filled their little black book with speciality roasters who regularly guest on the grinders (the house coffee is roasted by Origin in Cornwall).

SOCIETY'S TIP — GUEST ROASTS COME FROM AS NEARBY AS ROUND HILL IN SOMERSET AND AS FAR AS BAILIES IN BELFAST

The Corridor's tiny set-up means that most who cross its beautifully designed threshold are grabbing a coffee to sip while sauntering around the shops or to drink at their desk. However, those who decide to sit awhile at the window bar are treated to wonderful views over Bath Abbey and the Guildhall.

A crew of slick baristas ensure the queue keeps moving during the pre-work rush, although the short wait is the perfect moment to catch up on the latest beans or take your pick from the pastry selection.

ESTABLISHED
2014

KEY ROASTER
Origin Coffee Roasters

BREWING METHOD
Espresso, AeroPress, batch brew, cold brew

MACHINE
La Marzocco Linea PB

GRINDER
Mahlkonig Tanzania, Mahlkonig EK43, Nuova Simonelli Mythos x 2

OPENING HOURS
Mon-Sat 7.30am-6.30pm
Sun 9am-6pm

Gluten FREE

BEANS AVAILABLE / INSTORE

WIFI

CYCLE FRIENDLY

OUTDOOR seating

FAMILY FRIENDLY

DISABLED ACCESS

BRING YOUR OWN Cup

www.society-cafe.com   T: 01225 428008

f @societycafebath   🐦 @societycafe   📷 @societycafe

52 MOKOKO COFFEE – SOUTHGATE

7 Dorchester Street, Southgate, Bath, BA1 1SS

Bringing a sunny San Fran vibe to Bath, Mokoko beckons travellers bustling to and from the train station with its twinkly lights and resist-me-if-you-can aromas.

Peer longingly through the large front window to see shelves lined with bags of beans and brewing kit, while baristas busy themselves behind the bar extracting espresso on the gleaming Conti Monte Carlo machine.

TIP HATS OFF TO BARISTA CARL WHO IS THE UK AEROPRESS CHAMPION 2018

Coffee is something of an art form here, while the syphon method looks (to the uninitiated) more like a science experiment than an exercise in brewing. But they keep it fun, never precious – even when it comes to the tasting notes for the latest house-roasted beans.

Attention-to-detail coffee may be Mokoko's main attraction, but don't underestimate the cake. All baked in the newest Mokoko outpost in Bristol, the traybakes and tarts make it hard to choose. Hot picks from the daily line-up include the banging cinnamon swirl and creative range of chelsea buns.

ESTABLISHED
2014

KEY ROASTER
Mokoko

BREWING METHOD
Espresso, Kalita Wave, syphon, drip

MACHINE
Conti Monte Carlo

GRINDER
Mahlkonig EK43, Compak E10 Master

OPENING HOURS
Mon-Sat 7am-6pm
Sun 9am-6pm

 Gluten FREE

 BEANS AVAILABLE INSTORE

 WIFI

 OUTDOOR Seating

 DISABLED ACCESS

 BRING YOUR OWN Cup

www.mokokocoffee.com   T: 01225 333444
f @mokokocoffee   @mokokocoffee   @mokokocoffee

MAP № 53 YEO VALLEY HQ

Rhodyate, Blagdon, Somerset, BS40 7YE

Yeo Valley's canteen may have started out as a staff perk, but word soon spread that: a) the food was pretty spectacular, b) the views over the Somerset countryside were magnificent and c) the coffee was way above average.

So the team bowed to pressure to share these delights with the public, and now the delightfully funky space also serves local caffeine lovers and day-tripping lunchers alongside the Yeo Valley workforce.

As you'd expect from the home of some of the UK's best organic products, the espresso, filter and french press brews from Bristol roaster Extract are crafted to do justice to the top-notch house milk.

INSIDER'S TIP KEEP AN EYE OPEN FOR POP-UP DINNERS, FARM TOURS AND FOOD DEMOS

Kickstart the day with an espresso and brekkie of scotch pancakes oozing with yogurt and fruit compote.

A little later, plump for a post-lunch americano, which makes a perfect finale to hearty rustic dishes based around the farm's own organic meat, dairy and garden veg (visit on Wednesdays for the own-reared roast).

ESTABLISHED
2015

KEY ROASTER
Extract Coffee Roasters

BREWING METHOD
Espresso, filter, french press

MACHINE
S5 Compact ED

GRINDER
Mazzer Lux

OPENING HOURS
Tue-Fri 8.30am-5pm

Gluten FREE

WIFI

CYCLE FRIENDLY

OUTDOOR seating

DISABLED & ACCESS

BRING YOUR OWN cup.

---

www.yeovalley.co.uk   T: 01761 461425

f @yeovalley   🐦 @yeovalley   📷 @yeovalley

MAP № 54 STRANGERS WITH COFFEE

31 St Cuthbert Street, Wells, Somerset, BA5 2AW

Nobody stays a stranger for very long at this popular Wells institution. From new wave bean-buffs to caffeine-craving locals dropping in for a brew to-go, everyone receives a warm welcome and as much coffee and chat as they would like to engage in.

Tom Lowe and Jerry Naish, who recently took over the cafe from Ivan and Susan Hewitt, decided it was a no-brainer to continue with the hugely popular house blend and simple, locally sourced food ethos – albeit with their own fun twist.

TIP PAIR A COLD BREW SODA WITH A GENEROUS SLAB OF THE BERRY OAT BAR

'The customers love the Allpress Espresso Blend – at least once a week we have to promise not to change it,' says Jerry. 'We also always have three guest roasts rotating on filter to keep things fun for our customers – and for Tom.'

While Tom plays frontman and knows all the regulars, Jerry ensures there is always something seasonal on a menu of coffee shop classics which includes scrumptiously good sausage rolls and Strangers' special beans on toast.

ESTABLISHED
2012

KEY ROASTER
Allpress Espresso

BREWING METHOD
Espresso, V60

MACHINE
La Marzocco

GRINDER
Victoria Arduino Mythos One

OPENING HOURS
Tue-Sat **7.30**am-**4**pm

 Gluten FREE

 BEANS AVAILABLE
 INSTORE

 OUTDOOR seating

 BRING YOUR OWN Cup.

T: 07729 226200

f @strangerswithcoffee

MAP № 55 THE RIVER HOUSE

7 The Bridge, Frome, Somerset, BA11 1AR

If you're searching for a little pick-me-up, a trip to Frome's friendliest cafe, The River House, will certainly pep up your spirits.

There's not much that the happy-go-lucky team take seriously – though they make an exception for coffee. The in-house roast, Loud Mouth, champions *'gobby coffee not knobby coffee'* and aims to burst the bubble of caffeine snobbery in the creation of a brew that's light-hearted and downright delicious at the same time.

The foodie offering also bears the colourful River House stamp, and caff classics are funked up with creative quirks (try the Pigs and Cheese – oozy rarebit with bacon jam and a poached egg). Everything's made in-house, including the stuffed doughnuts served on Funky Hat Friday.

INSIDER'S TIP FLASH THE BARISTA A SMILE AND YOU MAY GET YOUR NAME ARTILY INSCRIBED ON YOUR LATTE

While day-to-day dealings are pleasingly laid back, the cafe's commitment to sustainability is also taken pretty seriously: packaging is recycled or biodegradable and you'll save some pennies on your takeaway drink if you pack a reusable cup.

ESTABLISHED
2014

KEY ROASTER
Loud Mouth Coffee

BREWING METHOD
Espresso, cold brew

MACHINE
Astoria Plus

GRINDER
Cimbali Magnum

OPENING HOURS
Mon-Fri 8am-6pm
Sat 9am-6pm
Sun 10am-4pm

www.riverhousefrome.co.uk   T: 01373 464847

f @theriverhousefrome   @riverhousefrome

MAP № 56 MOO AND TWO

27 Catherine Hill, Frome, Somerset, BA11 1BY

If you're seeking a zen space to savour incredible caffeine and catch up on a little me-time, file this Frome indie under your 'coffee shops to visit solo' list.

Owner Euan champions carefully brewed loose-leaf tea and makes an annual trip to India to source the finest organic crops for his lengthy line-up of tisanes. The wild nettle and mint is particularly restorative if you've come in search of calm.

INSIDER'S TIP CHECK OUT THE PERSONALISED MUGS – YOU'LL NEVER AGAIN GET THE OFFICE TEA ORDER WRONG

Just as consciously curated is the coffee, which is currently bronzed by local roastery Break Fluid. It's perfectly paired with the flaky all-butter pastries which are another product of Frome's thriving indie scene and crafted down the road at Rye Bakery.

Euan's continued to organically develop Moo and Two this year and has introduced pop-up plant shop PILEA, which has brought vibrant green flora to the pared-back brick and wood decor.

Keep up to date with regular plant workshops, supper clubs and live music events via social media.

ESTABLISHED
2016

KEY ROASTER
Break Fluid
Coffee Co.

BREWING METHOD
Espresso,
V60, AeroPress,
french press

MACHINE
La Spaziale S5

GRINDER
Mazzer Super
Jolly

OPENING HOURS
Tue-Sat 9am-5pm
(market first Sunday of the month)

Gluten FREE

BEANS AVAILABLE
INSTORE

WIFI

CYCLE FRIENDLY

OUTDOOR seating

FAMILY friendly

BRING YOUR OWN cup

---

www.mooandtwo.com   T: 07816 311452

f @mooandtwo   🐦 @moo_and_two   📷 @mooandtwo

DEVELOPED WITH BARISTAS FOR BARISTAS

- Perfect for latte art
- No added sugar
- Cholesterol free, low fat alternative to milk
- 30% less calories than skimmed & regular soy milk

UNSWEETENED

BLUE DIAMOND ALMONDS

Almond Breeze

Serving Suggestion

Rich & Creamy

BARISTA BLEND
Created for Use by Professionals
Dairy and Soya Free

Baristas know their coffee better than anyone. That's why we got baristas to help us make our new, low calorie Almond Breeze® Barista Blend. It's deliciously creamy and frothy, making it perfect for the world's finest coffee. And because it's an almond drink, it's dairy free and soya free

For more information & stockists visit **bluediamondalmonds.co.uk**

MAP№ 57 FINCA – YEOVIL

11 High Street, Yeovil, Somerset, BA20 1RG

This speciality spot in the centre of Yeovil is a dead cert for good coffee – not least because it's roasted by the Finca team themselves.

Choose between a caramel coloured crema-rich espresso which has been pulled through the La Marzocco or opt for a clean V60 or AeroPress. Then enjoy a moment savouring the subtle flavours of beans which have been carefully bronzed to enhance their specific profile.

TIP OUTDOOR TABLES DOUBLE THE SPACE, SO DON'T WORRY ABOUT GETTING A SEAT

A new 10kg Toper roaster has recently been installed at Finca's roastery at The Grove in Dorchester, to meet the increasing requirements of its Dorchester, Yeovil and Poundbury customers.

A DIY ethic runs throughout the business, so own-roasted coffee is accompanied by a creative collection of pastries, cakes and, recently, sourdough which are all crafted with equal attention to detail at Finca's bakery in Poundbury.

ESTABLISHED
2016

KEY ROASTER
Finca Coffee Roasters

BREWING METHOD
Espresso, V60, AeroPress, cold brew

MACHINE
La Marzocco

GRINDER
Olympus, Mazzer

OPENING HOURS
Mon-Sat **8**am-**4**pm
Sun **10**am-2pm

 Gluten FREE

 BEANS AVAILABLE / INSTORE

 OUTDOOR Seating

 DISABLED ACCESS

 COFFEE COURSES

ROASTERS

BATH & SOMERSET

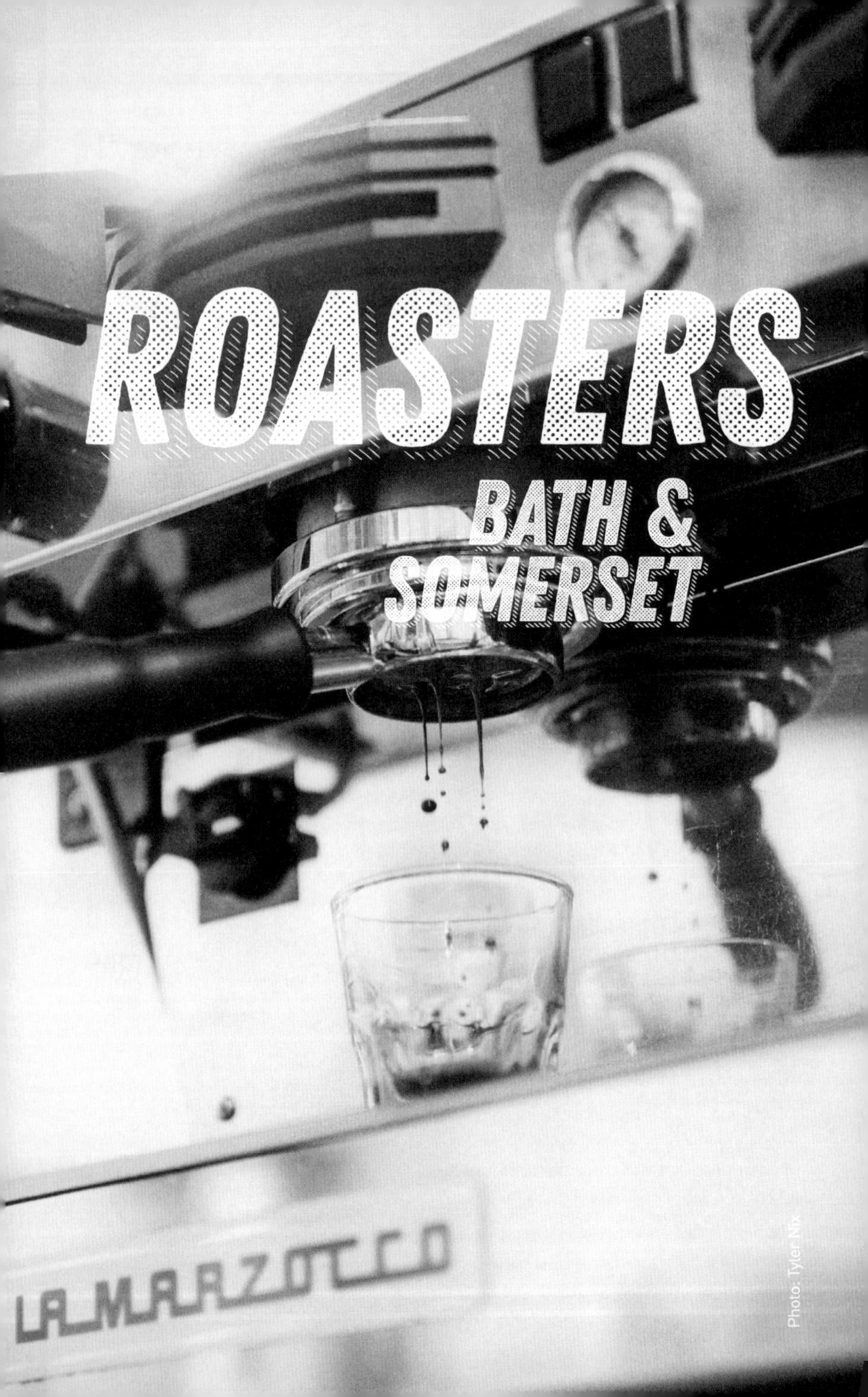

Photo: Tyler Nix

LA MARZOCCO

MAP 58 FAR SIDE COFFEE

The Welsh Mill, Park Hill Drive, Frome, Somerset, BA11 2LE

ESTABLISHED
2017

COLD BREW +NITRO AVAILABLE

ONLINE

ONSITE

Knowing cold brew had the potential to be beautifully complex, but unsatisfied by what was on offer, Kadie Regan set about making her own. It's a simple recipe: coffee + water + patience = cold brew, though scratch the surface and there's way more going on than first meets the eye.

Coffee from high altitude Peruvian and Rwandan plantations is carefully sourced for exquisite quality which translates into an intense drink with a refreshing kick.

'ALL OF FAR SIDE'S BEANS COME COURTESY OF FEMALE GROWERS'

All of Far Side's beans come courtesy of female growers who are supported by women's coffee alliances. These initiatives open the doors for women to develop skills, own coffee businesses and receive a fair price for their produce.

Kadie's cold brew process steeps single origin beans in filtered water for 18 hours and – leaving no flavour unextracted – results in contrasting punchy and subtle flavour notes. The Peruvian brew is bold with hints of sweet orange; the Rwandan a mash-up of maple and lemon with a cacao flourish. Sip them slowly to savour hidden depths.

www.farsidecoffee.com   T: 07711 846678

f @farsidecoffee   🐦 @farsidecoffee   📷 @farsidecoffee

MAP №59 BRAZIER COFFEE COMPANY

Unit 10, Tonedale Mill Business Park, Wellington, Somerset, TA21 0AW

S omerset's high altitude coffee specialist is hitting new heights in 2018 via some exciting developments. The roasting – which takes place on a Giesen WA6 in the Wellington cafe roastery – is about to be elevated further with the arrival of a big brother Giesen A30.

It'll be cooking up coffee sourced from across the world and, in particular, beans that are the result of Brazier's special relationship with Kinini in Rwanda.

Then there's the refurbishment of a three-storey listed building (in addition to the two cafe sites), and the employment of an exec chef who has worked with the likes of Gordon Ramsay.

'THE ROASTING IS ABOUT TO BE ELEVATED WITH THE ARRIVAL OF A GIESEN A30'

Cafes that work with Brazier are also benefiting: a new engineering division – with workshop and full-time engineers on the road – has been launched so machine glitches can be sorted speedily. *'We genuinely care about our customers,'* says Brazier owner, Tom. *'We tailor the coffee to them, provide details of our ethical sourcing and traceability, offer training in layout, workflow and barista skills and even supply, install and maintain equipment.'*

ESTABLISHED
2015

ROASTER
MAKE & SIZE
Giesen WA6

CAFE ONSITE

OPEN TO THE PUBLIC

COFFEE COURSES

BEANS AVAILABLE
ONLINE ONSITE

www.braziercoffeeroasters.co.uk   T: 01823 666585

f @braziercoffeeroasters   🐦 @brazierroasters   📷 @braziercoffeeroasters

WILTSHIRE & DORSET

№61
SOUTH COAST ROAST

*All locations are approximate

67

Lyme Regis   Bridport

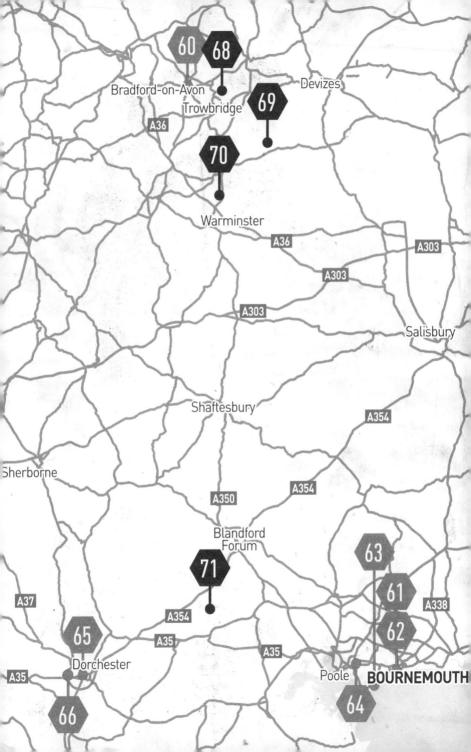

MAP № 60 GILOU'S

4 The Shambles, Bradford-on-Avon, Wiltshire, BA15 1JS

Speciality coffee served with a soupçon of French flair is what makes this community cafe in Bradford-on-Avon so popular.

The cafe menu du jour calls upon various roasters of reputation (Origin, Colonna, Round Hill and Bailies to name a few) and keeps bean buffs buoyant with anticipation about what will feature next in the hopper.

TIP BEAN BURN OUT? TURN YOUR ATTENTION TO THE GREAT SELECTION OF COMINS TEA

On the food front, influences of Gallic gastronomy are present in the temptress-like tartines (toppings include beetroot pesto and mature cheddar), an array of gorgeous gateaux (the gluten-free dark and white chocolate and almond cake is knockout), exquisite viennoiserie (try the almond croissant) and delicious desserts (the mousse au chocolat disappears fast). Veggies are well looked after across the board.

The cafe regularly holds fundraisers for Bristol charity For-ethiopia, while industrial-chic lighting and a Bath-stone wall make an interesting backdrop for quirky local art.

ESTABLISHED
2016

KEY ROASTER
Origin Coffee Roasters

BREWING METHOD
Espresso, V60, AeroPress

MACHINE
Sanremo Zoe

GRINDER
Mythos One Clima Pro, Mazzer

OPENING HOURS
Mon 10am-5pm
Thu-Sun 10am-5pm

 Gluten FREE

 BEANS AVAILABLE INSTORE

 WIFI

 CYCLE FRIENDLY

 OUTDOOR SEATING

 FAMILY FRIENDLY

 DISABLED ACCESS

 BRING YOUR OWN Cup

www.gilouscafe.com T: 01225 862203

f @Gilou's @gilouscafe

MAP №61 SOUTH COAST ROAST

24 Richmond Hill, Bournemouth, Dorset, BH2 6EJ

With stripped-back brickwork and gleaming tiles, South Coast Roast brings a blast of Aussie coffee culture to up-town Bournemouth. The buoyant attitude of the ever-welcoming staff makes it a go-to for locals seeking a place to kick back and take in a low-key buzz.

Simplicity, inclusivity and attention to detail are SCR's top priorities. Pretentiousness and coffee snobbery don't make the list. Bad Hand supplies the house roast, with guest V60s and batch brews sourced from Caravan and Full Circle among others. Mindful of the science of coffee, manager James Harris sees the beans as raw ingredients to be coaxed and crafted into superlative brews. A finer-than-average grind is used to achieve consistently super-sweet notes.

TIP THE VEGAN GLUTEN-FREE BROWNIE IS FAST GAINING A CULT FOLLOWING

Inspired by Cambodia's Vibe Cafe, tempting vegan food gets high billing. Meaty dishes have plant-based alternatives that make vegan fare accessible but not preachy. Look out for the scrambled tofu or hearty 'Bodia bowls' – generous salads packed with goodies which smack of deliciousness over virtue.

ESTABLISHED
2007

KEY ROASTER
Bad Hand
Coffee

BREWING METHOD
Espresso, V60,
batch brew,
Clever Dripper

MACHINE
La Marzocco
Linea 2

GRINDER
Mahlkonig K30

OPENING HOURS
Mon-Fri 8am-5pm
Sat 9am-5pm
Sun 9am-4pm

 Gluten FREE

 BEANS AVAILABLE INSTORE

 WIFI

 CYCLE FRIENDLY

 OUTDOOR seating

 FAMILY FRIENDLY

 DISABLED ACCESS

 BRING YOUR OWN Cup

 COFFEE COURSES

---

www.southcoastroastcafe.com T: 01202 551197

 f @southcoastroastcafe 🐦 @southcoastroast 📷 @southcoastroastcafe

^{MAP №}62 ESPRESSO KITCHEN

69 Commercial Road, Bournemouth, Dorset, BH2 5RT

No need to grab a newspaper if you forget to pack reading material on your visit to this Bournemouth indie as every inch of the cafe – including the ceiling – is decorated with eye-catching finds from the team's travels.

Grab a spot on the bench downstairs, take in the stimulating surrounds and watch the team perfect intricate latte art. Alternatively, head up to the cosy den on the first floor and scribble your praise for the barista's swan skills on the chalkboard wall.

TIP GET DOWN WITH THE DIRTY CHAI: DOUBLE ESPRESSO, NATURAL SPICES AND FOAMED MILK

Speciality beans for these milky masterpieces are sourced from local roaster Beanpress, which craft the cafe's signature house blend. If you want to sample something different, there's also a weekly-changing single origin espresso from a range of South West roasters.

Plant-based and raw food followers, organic fans and gluten dodgers will be happy to hear that Espresso Kitchen's foodie offering has expanded to include even more vibrant options – try the vegan cheese toasties followed by a hefty slice of the famous carrot cake.

ESTABLISHED
2012

KEY ROASTER
Beanpress
Coffee Co.

BREWING METHOD
Espresso

MACHINE
La Marzocco
FB70

GRINDER
La Marzocco
Swift

OPENING HOURS
Mon-Sat 7am-7pm
Sun 9am-6pm

 Gluten FREE

 BEANS AVAILABLE INSTORE

 WIFI

 OUTDOOR seating

 BRING YOUR OWN cup.

 COFFEE COURSES

---

www.espressokitchen.co.uk   T: 01202 942420

f @espressokitchen   @espressokitchen

MAP № 63 COFFEE SALOON

9 Haven Road, Canford Cliffs, Poole, Dorset, BH13 7LE

offee Saloon's Canford Cliffs cafe is the HQ of its stable of speciality shops (voted the second best coffee houses in Dorset by the *Bournemouth Echo*) which range across the wild West Country.

To take them all in, saddle your steed and gallop from Westbourne to Weymouth, stopping to wet your whistle in Poole, Wareham and Dorchester.

At each quirkily-decorated saloon, you'll be greeted by a friendly team of espresso-slinging baristas who craft a mean brew from beans fired in Cornwall by Origin.

INSIDER TIP WITH SWANKY SANDBANKS NEARBY, THIS IS A GREAT PLACE FOR COFFEE-FUELLED CELEB SPOTTING

A hoedown at the headquarters revolves around excellent espresso and locally sourced and homemade food. The avo on sourdough with lime and chilli flakes is a fave savoury, while a bijou baking kitchen at the rear rustles up gorgeous goodies such as vegan banana bread and chocolate orange brownies.

Some of the best seats are to be found on the south-facing decking, or it's just a short trot to the beach with your coffee to-go.

ESTABLISHED
2014

KEY ROASTER
Origin Coffee Roasters

BREWING METHOD
Espresso

MACHINE
La Marzocco

GRINDER
Mythos One Clima Pro

OPENING HOURS
Mon-Fri **7**am-**4**pm
Sat-Sun **8**am-**4**pm

Gluten FREE

BEANS AVAILABLE INSTORE

WIFI

CYCLE FRIENDLY

OUTDOOR seating

FAMILY FRIENDLY

DISABLED ACCESS

BRING YOUR OWN cup.

COFFEE COURSES

---

www.coffeesaloon.com   T: 07384 110486

f @coffeesaloon   @ @thecoffeesaloons

MAP №64 LITTLE RED ROASTER

18 Station Road, Parkstone, Poole, Dorset, BH14 8UB

New Yorkers preach that black coffee and bagels are the only way to start the day, and the team at this Poole coffee shop certainly champion the breakfast tradition with their daily line-up of the duo.

A new generation of the Roberts family has taken over the Parkstone cafe, and with them has come a (little red) roaster which fills the air with the intoxicating scent of gently bronzing coffee.

Exclusive single origins are the beans of choice and are roasted in small batches to ensure every cup is lip-smackingly fresh. Dorset's Beanpress Coffee Co. provide the house espresso which is served via the Conti Monte Carlo machine, while a Bunn single-cup brewer squeezes the best flavour profiles from the beans.

TIP
INSIDER **LRR IS MUTT-FRIENDLY SO GIVE THE DOG A RUN ON ASHLEY CROSS GREEN BEFORE SWINGING BY**

Sourdough bagels are fresh from a local bakery and stuffed with delicious local ingredients. Cram in a homemade cake too (if you're made of stern stuff) and don't forget to replenish your stock of beans from the retail selection before heading home.

ESTABLISHED
2010

KEY ROASTER
Beanpress Coffee Co.

BREWING METHOD
Espresso, batch brew, Bunn Trifecta

MACHINE
Conti Monte Carlo

GRINDER
Anfim SCODY

OPENING HOURS
Mon-Fri 7am-5pm
Sat 8am-5pm
Sun 9am-2pm

Gluten FREE

BEANS AVAILABLE
INSTORE

WIFI

BRING YOUR OWN *Cup*

---

www.littleredroaster.co.uk   T: 01202 240450

f @littleredcoffee   @littleredroaster

MAP №65 FINCA – DORCHESTER

41 Great Western Road, Dorchester, Dorset, DT1 1UF

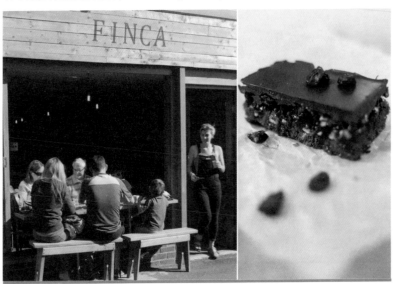

Folk in Dorchester are well blessed with coffee shops and places to eat but, for the speciality coffee fan, the go-to has always been Finca.

This bijou and rustic cafe, which recently won Coffee Shop of the Year in the Dorset Food and Drink Awards, has become a home from home for the loyal band of regulars who visit from morning through to teatime.

INSIDER'S TIP NAB A SEAT AT THE BIFOLDING WINDOWS AND WATCH THE WORLD GO BY AS YOU SIP YOUR WELL-MADE BREW

Head to the counter to place your order and, in addition to the gleaming La Marzocco machine, you'll find a stonking selection of homemade bakes and cakes that switches with the seasons. Ask the baristas for the latest own-roasted coffee and cake pairing recommendations.

The team have also recently started making sourdough at the Finca bakery in Poundbury. Delight in it via one of the lunchtime toasties (the creative fillings are fab).

ESTABLISHED
2014

KEY ROASTER
Finca Coffee Roasters

BREWING METHOD
Espresso, V60, AeroPress, cold brew

MACHINE
La Marzocco

GRINDER
Olympus, Mazzer

OPENING HOURS
Mon-Sat 9am-4pm
Sun 10am-2pm

Gluten FREE

BEANS AVAILABLE INSTORE

OUTDOOR seating

DISABLED ACCESS

COFFEE COURSES

---

www.fincacoffee.co.uk T: 01305 300400

f @fincadorchester 🐦 @scouting4coffee 📷 @scouting4coffee

№66 FINCA – POUNDBURY

The Buttercross, Poundbury, Dorchester, Dorset, DT1 3AZ

The third and youngest member of the Finca family turns out to be the big brother when it comes to capacity.

Set in the iconic Buttermarket in Poundbury, the roomy spot serves its own-roasted coffee from beans cooked up on a new 10kg Toper at The Grove in Dorchester.

In keeping with the Finca ethos of making everything from scratch, the sourdough, bakes and cakes are crafted by the team on-site, so you won't find anywhere for miles with such authentically fresh-from-the-roaster/oven delights.

TIP NITRO COLD BREW CHANGES TO REFLECT THE HOUSE-ROASTED SEASONAL COFFEES

The Poundbury outpost also has chilled and creamy nitro cold brew on tap which, coupled with the outdoor seating, makes this spot an absolute must-visit on sunny days.

Swing by for lunch, grab a bierkeller table and sink your teeth into a sarnie from the new range – followed by coffee and cake, of course.

ESTABLISHED
2017

KEY ROASTER
Finca Coffee Roasters

BREWING METHOD
Espresso, V60, AeroPress, nitro cold brew

MACHINE
La Marzocco

GRINDER
Olympus

OPENING HOURS
Mon-Sat 8am-4pm
Sun 10am-2pm

 Gluten FREE

 BEANS AVAILABLE INSTORE

 OUTDOOR seating

 FAMILY FRIENDLY

 DISABLED ACCESS

 COFFEE COURSES

---

www.fincacoffee.co.uk   T: 01305 300400

f @fincapoundbury   🐦 @scouting4coffee   📷 @scouting4coffee

MAP 67 AMID GIANTS AND IDOLS

59 Silver Street, Lyme Regis, Dorset, DT7 3HR

Whether you're seeking refuge from Lyme's school-holiday frenzy or foot-weary after a blustery stroll along the Cobb, Amid Giants and Idols offers caffeine-scented sanctuary.

The laid-back surroundings have a front-room vibe with comfy chairs, the soothing sizzle of the steam wand and board games inviting visitors to linger over just-one-more coffee. Opt for the home-roasted house blend, Coast, or savour a single origin option from Crankhouse or Brazier.

TIP ASK OWNERS STEVE AND ELAINE FOR THE BEST BREW METHOD TO MATCH THE LATEST GUEST BEANS

Additional guest roasteries such as Yallah crop up from time to time to keep the regulars on their toes, while the option of woodneck or AeroPress alongside espresso caters for filter fans. It's worth asking the barista to recommend what's best for a V60 that day.

Tempting bakes of the fruity and chocolatey variety are homemade and hard to take a pass on, while vibrant salads and thickly cut sarnies make a more substantial snack for visitors heading onwards to the South West Coast Path.

ESTABLISHED
2014

KEY ROASTER
Multiple roasters

BREWING METHOD
Espresso, V60, AeroPress, woodneck

MACHINE
La Marzocco Linea

GRINDER
Mazzer

OPENING HOURS
Mon-Sun 10am-4pm

www.amidgiantsandidols.co.uk   T: 01297 443791

WILTSHIRE & DORSET
ROASTERS

MAP No. 68 DUSTY APE COFFEE ROASTERS

Marsh Farm Roastery, Hilperton, Wiltshire, BA14 7PJ

The Dusty Ape crew are scouring the globe for the best beans that'll deliver the horizon-expanding flavours they require – and few corners of the coffee-farming world remain untouched.

In a United Nations of bean bronzing, Nicaragua rubs shoulders with Ethiopia, Peru and Sumatra. Yet however wide the sourcing net is cast, quality is always the focus: cherries which have been triple-picked for defects and ripeness aren't unheard of.

'GOD FORGIVES THOSE WHO DRINK CARAMEL LATTES, PROVIDED THEY'RE MADE FROM GOOD COFFEE,' SAYS PHIL

With beans secured, Dusty Ape then coax out the distinctive flavours. The chief persuaders are a 5kg Toper and a 12kg Probat. Small-batch hand roasting and meticulous profiling ensure roasts can be reliably reproduced and guarantee that every cup of the house blends, Silverback and Molten Toffee, hit the spot.

Knowing that only so many coffees can be consumed in a day, the Wiltshire roastery aims to make each one a stonker and they're not snooty about how you choose to drink it. 'We now stock syrups because apparently God forgives those who drink caramel lattes, provided they're made from good coffee', says founder Phil Buckley.

ESTABLISHED
2013

ROASTER
MAKE & SIZE
Toper 5kg
Probat 12kg

CAFE ONSITE

OPEN BY APPOINTMENT

BEANS AVAILABLE
ONLINE ONSITE

www.dustyape.com T: 01225 753838
f @dustyapecoffee @dustyape @dustyape

MAP 69 SQUARE ROOT COFFEE ROASTERY

12 Station Yard, Edington, Wiltshire, BA13 4NT

It's hard to stress just how much attention to detail goes into each cup crafted by Adrian Smith, master roaster at Wiltshire's Square Root Coffee.

Firstly, there are the fresh greens which can be traced back to the fields where they were grown and the farmers who grew them (paid above market value so they can invest in their own infrastructure).

Then there's the endless exploration of the taste nuances within each lot, the sample roasting to find the sweet spot and the cupping of samples until a perfectly roasted beauty emerges.

Once the team is happy, the coffee is roasted in small batches on a custom-made Turkish roaster named Laura.

'THE COFFEE IS ROASTED IN SMALL BATCHES ON A CUSTOM-MADE TURKISH ROASTER NAMED LAURA'

Beans are always bronzed to suit a particular brewing method and serve style, which is why the signature espresso blend, The Solution, with its Brazilian-Indian-Sumatran origins, tastes sublime in milk-based drinks as well as on its own for a smooth morning pick-me-up.

ESTABLISHED
2015

ROASTER
MAKE & SIZE
TX5 5kg

OPEN
BY APPOINTMENT

BEANS
AVAILABLE

ONLINE

www.squarerootcoffee.com   T: 07940 120835

f @squarerootcoffee   🐦 @sqrootcoffee

MAP:70 GIRLS WHO GRIND COFFEE

Unit 2, Millards Farm, Upton Scudamore, Wiltshire, BA12 0AQ

R epping the incredible females who fuel the speciality movement, Fiona O'Brien and Casey Lalonde launched Girls Who Grind in October 2017 to offer an alternative to the male-dominated coffee scene.

Women make up over 50 per cent of the coffee farming workforce, but are often under-acknowledged and underpaid. So this girl-power gang is supporting them by only roasting coffees grown by female producers and working with organisations that support and empower them.

ESTABLISHED
2017

ROASTER
MAKE & SIZE
Giesan W6A

OPEN
BY APPOINTMENT

BEANS
AVAILABLE
ONLINE   OFFSITE

'WOMEN MAKE UP OVER 50 PER CENT OF THE COFFEE FARMING WORKFORCE'

The dynamic duo – Casey previously roasted in Vermont while Fi designed kickass branding and crafted incredible coffee back home in Melbourne – blend their experience to produce a beautifully-packaged selection of seasonal small batch beans.

Single origins from the Wiltshire roastery have so far included an incredible Kenya AA Gichuna Kiambu and their first Sisterhood Relationship Coffee, which is sourced from three sisters in El Salvador.

www.girlswhogrindcoffee.com   T: 01985 211151
f @girlswhogrindcoffee   🐦 @gwg_coffee   📷 @girlswhogrindcoffee

MAP № 71 BEANPRESS COFFEE CO.

The Old Stables, North West Farm, Winterborne Kingston, Dorset, DT11 9AT

For the past five years, globetrotting roaster Ben Roberts has tasted his way around the world on a quest to source beans for his cast iron Joper.

So far he's racked up air miles travelling to organic coffee farms in Ethiopia, Brazil, Guatemala and Nicaragua where he's formed solid relationships with farmers who grow the greens destined for his Dorset roastery.

'WE HAND-PACK EACH CAN AND FLUSH THE BEANS WITH NITROGEN FOR OPTIMUM FRESHNESS'

It's not all play and no work for the Beanpress founder though as he's also been busy developing fresh packaging for his speciality coffee. Ben believes the new recyclable and refillable metal cans are not only eco-conscious but also yield an even fresher cup: *'We hand-pack each can and flush the beans with nitrogen for optimum freshness.'*

When Ben and the team aren't busy roasting beans for their crew of wholesale customers and reducing waste with eco-friendly packaging, you'll often find them sharing their knowledge with the coffee-curious folk who sign up for the on-site coffee courses.

ESTABLISHED
2013

ROASTER
MAKE & SIZE
Joper BPR-25

OPEN BY APPOINTMENT

COFFEE COURSES

COURSES

BEANS AVAILABLE

ONLINE

www.beanpress.co.uk T: 01929 472666
f @beanpresscoffee @beanpresscoffee

DEVON

№85
ALMOND THIEF BAKERY

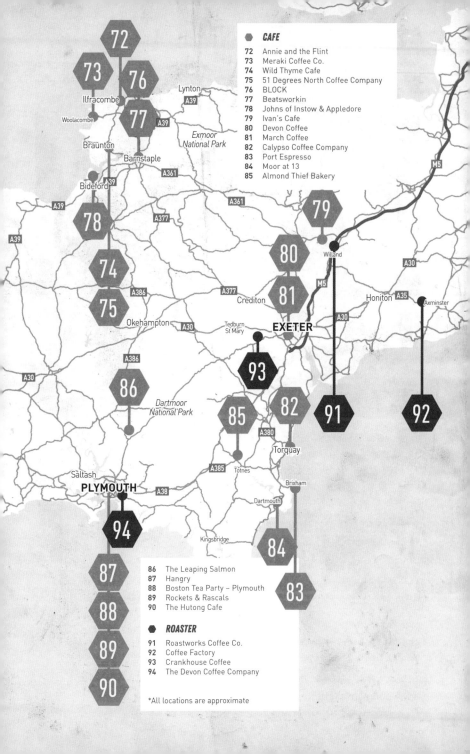

CAFE

72 Annie and the Flint
73 Meraki Coffee Co.
74 Wild Thyme Cafe
75 51 Degrees North Coffee Company
76 BLOCK
77 Beatsworkin
78 Johns of Instow & Appledore
79 Ivan's Cafe
80 Devon Coffee
81 March Coffee
82 Calypso Coffee Company
83 Port Espresso
84 Moor at 13
85 Almond Thief Bakery

86 The Leaping Salmon
87 Hangry
88 Boston Tea Party – Plymouth
89 Rockets & Rascals
90 The Hutong Cafe

ROASTER

91 Roastworks Coffee Co.
92 Coffee Factory
93 Crankhouse Coffee
94 The Devon Coffee Company

*All locations are approximate

MAP No. 72 ANNIE AND THE FLINT

126 High Street, Ilfracombe, Devon, EX34 9EY

When it comes to coffee compatibility, it's good to know your type. Luckily, the team at Annie and the Flint are always on hand with advice and will happily match you with a speciality sip to satisfy your senses.

Whether you've a penchant for one that is rich, dark and handsome or have a thing for a medium body with a long sweet finish, the list of Origin-roasted espresso based drinks will woo your palate.

As will the health-conscious food offering. This industrial-chic joint offers everything from salads of roasted broccoli, pine nuts and feta to pancake brekkies with yogurt, compote and berries.

INSIDER'S TIP COFFEE OVERLOAD? GIVE THE CHAI, TURMERIC OR EARL GREY LATTE A WHIRL

On a superfood health kick? The peanut butter energy truffles – stuffed with dates, coconut oil and oats – pack a nutritious punch, especially when combined with a Purple Blast smoothie of blueberries, pomegranate and organic yogurt.

And don't forget to grab a bag of beans and a jar of honey from the shop on your way out.

ESTABLISHED
2016

KEY ROASTER
Origin Coffee Roasters

BREWING METHOD
Espresso

MACHINE
La Marzocco

GRINDER
Mythos One

OPENING HOURS
Mon-Fri 8.30am-4.30pm
Sat 9am-4pm

Gluten FREE

BEANS AVAILABLE INSTORE

WIFI

FAMILY FRIENDLY

DISABLED ACCESS

BRING YOUR OWN Cup.

www.annieandtheflint.co.uk   T: 01271 866436

f @annieandtheflint   @annieandtheflint

MAP 73 MERAKI COFFEE CO.

12 South Street, Woolacombe, Devon, EX34 7BB

This side-street gem is just a salty-haired dash from Woolacombe's sandy shore.

Self-taught baristas and owners Anthony Merret and Rohan Molligoda took over the former gallery at the start of 2018 and wasted no time in transforming the space into an easy-going coffee shop where sea-frolickers fill up on homemade specials and tourists escape the bustle for a quality caffeine fix.

When he's not bobbing about in the surf, you'll find Anthony slinging Devon Coffee espresso from the slick Astoria Storm machine which crowns the stainless-steel-top bar. The whole set-up is lovingly handcrafted (and all the more charming for it) with coastal photography, *Lonely Planet* guides and grinder parts referencing Meraki's holy trinity of caffeine, surf and community.

INSIDER'S TIP DON'T DOUBLE CHECK YOUR ORDER – THE DEVON COFFEE CO DECAF IS SO GOOD YOU WON'T TASTE THE DIFFERENCE

'We focus on three things here,' says Anthony, *'crafting great coffee, making people happy and creating a welcoming environment.'* A fitting focus for a cafe which is named after the Greek word that translates as *'love, soul and the creativity one puts into work'*.

ESTABLISHED
2018

KEY ROASTER
The Devon Coffee Company

BREWING METHOD
Espresso

MACHINE
Astoria Storm

GRINDER
Fiorenzato F83,
Fiorenzato F4
Fiorenzato F83
E XGi

OPENING HOURS
Mon-Sun 8am-4.30pm

Gluten FREE

BEANS AVAILABLE INSTORE

WIFI

FAMILY FRIENDLY

DISABLED ACCESS

BRING YOUR OWN Cup

T: 01271 871084

f @merakicoffeeco   @merakicoffeecompany

MAP 74 WILD THYME CAFE

5 Caen Field Shopping Centre, Braunton, Devon, EX33 1EE

Regular wave riders heading to north Devon's sandy beaches hardly need an introduction to this cool corner cafe in the nearby village of Braunton. It's long been a welcome staging post for beach-bound bods in need of a pre-surf coffee perk-up.

The offering is lip-smackingly fresh: organic Colombian beans from the cafe's own roastery, Kope, are ground to order and showcase notes of chocolate and toffee apple. A feature coffee, courtesy of Bristol's Clifton, rings the changes while a Brazilian single origin triple-filtered cold brew makes for summery refreshment.

INSIDER'S TIP: PICK UP A PACK OF FRESHLY ROASTED KOPE BEANS TO TAKE HOME

The cosy atmosphere encourages friendliness between surfers, holidaymakers and locals alike. The dawn patrol arrives early for smoothies and an all-day brekkie menu, locals gossip over globally-inspired lunches (with plenty of plant-based options), while idlers pop in to contemplate life over mocha and a slab of cake.

ESTABLISHED
2006

KEY ROASTER
Kope Coffee Roasters

BREWING METHOD
Espresso, cold brew

MACHINE
Astoria

GRINDER
Fiorenzato F38

OPENING HOURS
Mon-Sun 9am-4pm

 Gluten FREE

 BEANS AVAILABLE INSTORE

 WIFI

 CYCLE FRIENDLY

 OUTDOOR SEATING

 FAMILY FRIENDLY

 BRING YOUR OWN CUP

 COFFEE COURSES

---

www.wildthymecafe.co.uk   T: 01271 815191
f @wildthymecafe   🐦 @wildthymecafe   📷 @wildthymecafe

MAP 75 51 DEGREES NORTH COFFEE COMPANY

On the move in north Devon and at festivals across the South West

Speciality fans get used to going out of their way to pick up a quality coffee, and always have a list of local hotspots on their mental map. But if they're at a music festival in the middle of a field, a sporting event or even a wedding, the safest option is often a cup of tea.

Happily, however, a growing band of mobile coffee vans is taking speciality to the people. Quality espresso lovers in Braunton, for example, have learned to keep an eagle eye out for the 51 Degrees North Coffee Company van which pops up all over the place, including outside Tesco most weekday mornings, as well as at festivals and one-off events on the weekend.

INSIDER'S TIP MOCHA IS MADE WITH FRESHLY MELTED SINGLE ORIGIN CHOCOLATE AND STEAMED LOCAL MILK

Owner Justin Duerden uses Coffee Factory beans in his solar-power-assisted set-up and is also a Plastic Free North Devon Champion. Milk comes from a nearby farm via a refillable milk system and even the tea is blended locally and comes in biodegradable sachets. A percentage of the profits go to an animal rescue charity, too.

ESTABLISHED
2017

KEY ROASTER
The Coffee Factory

BREWING METHOD
Espresso, Clever Dripper, AeroPress, cold brew

MACHINE
Astoria Divina

GRINDER
Anfim SCODY II, Wilfa Svart

OPENING HOURS
Mon-Fri from **8**am
Sat-Sun **as per event**

---

www.51degreesnorthcoffee.com   T: 07403 944544
f @51degreesnorthcoffee   🐦 @51degnorthcc   📷 @51degreesnorthcoffee

№ 76 BLOCK

12-14 Butchers Row, Barnstaple, Devon, EX31 1BW

Barnstaple's hippest hangout serves up coffee to complement the quality of its eclectic global food and Northern Soul tunes.

Andy and Tran Stephenson gave up corporate life a year ago in order to create their dream cafe, and found a home among the quirky band of indies on historic Butchers Row. Neighbours include a top-notch cheese store, a game purveyor and a traditional fishmonger.

Caffeine fiends visit BLOCK for well-crafted coffee from Bristol roastery Clifton, which is served in a mismatch of retro 60s and 70s stoneware and china, ready to be perfectly paired with homemade cakes and cookies.

TIP DON'T MISS THE CRACKING MONTHLY SUPPER CLUBS WHICH OFFER A FEAST OF FUN COMMUNAL DINING

The Asian-influenced menu is the other reason to swing by – colourful bowls of ramen, bibimbap and poke are staples on a menu of regularly switched up contemporary dishes from across the globe.

ESTABLISHED
2017

KEY ROASTER
Clifton Coffee
Roasters

BREWING METHOD
Espresso

MACHINE
La Marzocco

GRINDER
Compak

OPENING HOURS
Tue-Sat **8**am-**5**pm

Gluten FREE

BEANS AVAILABLE INSTORE

WIFI

FAMILY FRIENDLY

BRING YOUR OWN Cup

www.eatatblock.com   T: 01271 342045

f @eatatblock   🐦 @eatatblock   📷 @eatatblock

MAP№ 77 BEATSWORKIN

9 Queen's House, Queen's Street, Barnstaple, Devon, EX32 8HJ

Beatsworkin's mix of coffee and skate culture may be unusual, but it's a super successful mash-up. And if you're a fan of the grind (of either variety, or simply curious), you'll be warmly welcomed.

The Beats gang have teamed up with Beanberry to secure a stonking supply of beans from across the globe. Roasted specifically for the house espresso, V60 and Chemex serve styles, it's crafted with care by the (skater) baristas who have been treated to some heavy duty training by the roaster.

It's this attention to detail, combined with owner Glenn Field's passion for doing everything well, that results in the high-quality cup.

₣TIP BAG A DISCOUNT FOR YOUR KEEPCUP AND PICK UP BEANS TO BREW AT HOME

Caffeinated tricks are complemented by a range of green smoothies, locally made bakes and milkshakes, with conscious reducing, reusing and recycling applied across the board.

ESTABLISHED
2015

KEY ROASTER
Beanberry
Coffee Company

BREWING METHOD
Espresso, filter,
Chemex, V60,
cold brew

MACHINE
Sanremo Verona
TCS

GRINDER
Mahlkonig K30 Air

OPENING HOURS
Mon-Fri **8.30**am-**6**pm
Sat **9**am-**6**pm
Sun **11**am-**4**pm

Gluten FREE

BEANS AVAILABLE INSTORE

WIFI

CYCLE FRIENDLY

 OUTDOOR seating

FAMILY FRiENDly

DISABLED ACCESS

BRING YOUR OWN *Cup*

COFFEE COURSES

---

www.beatsworkin.net   T: 01271 321111

f @Beatsworkin Coffee n Skate   🐦 @beatsworkinuk   📷 @beatsworkin

MAP 78 JOHNS OF INSTOW & APPLEDORE

6-7 The Quay, Appledore, Devon, EX39 1QS

For almost a century, locals have made a beeline for Johns for its cornucopia of South West produce and deli delights. And, since the family-owned stores and cafes (there's one of each on either side of the estuary at Appledore and Instow) teamed up with Roastworks at the start of 2018, it's also where they head for a decent cup of coffee.

TIP LOOK OUT FOR THEMED POP-UP EVENTS AND BRUNCH WITH LIVE MUSIC FROM LOCAL ARTISTS

Roasted in the heart of Devon, the Roastworks blend has won over the cafes' veteran coffee drinkers with its smooth notes of jammy sweetness and rich cocoa. Those tempted to take the indulgence up another notch plump for a mocha made with Willie's single origin cacao.

Stick around for brunch, lunch or afternoon tea and tuck in to homemade fare such as french toast with fruit compote and maple syrup, slow cooked pulled pork tacos and irresistibly gooey chocolate brownies.

You'll also find artisan goodies galore in the retail section – including Roastworks beans – so you can fashion brunch at home.

ESTABLISHED
1926

KEY ROASTER
Roastworks
Coffee Co.

BREWING METHOD
Espresso

MACHINE
Conti X-One

GRINDER
Mahlkonig K30
Vario

OPENING HOURS
Mon-Sun **8**am-**6**pm
(extended in summer)

Gluten FREE

BEANS AVAILABLE
INSTORE

WIFI

CYCLE FRIENDLY

OUTDOOR seating

FAMILY FRIENDLY

DISABLED ACCESS

BRING YOUR OWN Cup

---

www.johnsofinstow.co.uk   T: 01237 429065

f @johnsdelidevon   🐦 @johnsdelidevon   📷 @johnsdelidevon

MAP 79 IVAN'S CAFE

Halberton Court Farm Shop, High Street, Halberton, Devon, EX16 7AF

U nfortunately, when Geraint Thomas and Chris Froome whizzed through Halberton during the 2018 Tour of Britain they didn't have time to pop in to Ivan's speciality/cycling haven.

They missed out, because with its velo-themed decor (there's even a bike suspended from the old beams), mould-to-the-contours sofa and tasty seasonal dishes, this is an understandably popular pit stop for cyclists.

But it's not just sippers on spokes who make Ivan's their destination for a decent cup of coffee and locally sourced food. Dog walkers (it gets a round of appaws for being pooch friendly), locals and passing day trippers appreciate the careful crafting of Brazier beans roasted in nearby Wellington, alongside other South West stars including Roastworks, Crediton Coffee and Crankhouse.

TIP EXPLODING BAKERY TRAYBAKES AND CHUNK OF DEVON PIES PROVIDE SUSTENANCE FOR THOSE ON TWO WHEELS

When the weather is harsh and legs are cold, top-notch natural coffee on filter or crema-rich espresso is complemented by warming treats like roasted butternut squash, pancetta and feta chilli tart or Mexican bean frittata.

ESTABLISHED
2018

KEY ROASTER
Brazier Coffee Roasters

BREWING METHOD
Espresso, Technivorm Moccamaster

MACHINE
Sanremo Verde

GRINDER
Mahlkonig K30 Vario

OPENING HOURS
Tue-Fri 9am-4pm
Sat-Sun 10am-4pm
(reduced in autumn/winter)

 Gluten FREE

 BEANS AVAILABLE INSTORE

 WIFI

CYCLE FRIENDLY

OUTDOOR SEATING

FAMILY FRIENDLY

 DISABLED ACCESS

 BRING YOUR OWN Cup

www.ivanscafe.com   T: 01884 821458

f @ivanscoffee   🐦 @ivanscoffee   📷 @ivanscafe

MAP N°80 DEVON COFFEE

88 Queen Street, Exeter, Devon, EX4 3RP

Duck just off Exeter's main drag, follow your nose and you'll find yourself in the comforting embrace of Devon Coffee.

The bijou spot, all rustic decor and wood panelling, provides welcome relief in a city centre dominated by yet-more coffee chains. Open shelves form an elegantly dishevelled backdrop to the baristas as they set to their caffeine alchemy.

INSIDER'S TIP CHANNEL ITALIAN VIBES WITH AN AFFOGATO ON THE ALFRESCO SEATING

Thanks to the La Marzocco, the intense aroma of the seasonal house roast fills Devon Coffee's cosy interior. Bespoke beans come from Crankhouse which is based all of six miles away, while a second grinder allows guest appearances from regional and UK roasters such as Notes and Girls Who Grind.

V60 and AeroPress filters are available alongside nitro cold brew and batch brew, and there are also tumeric lattes, indulgent hot chocs and fragrant Canton teas if you've maxed out on coffee. Chase your choice with a bacon buttie, locally baked sourdough toastie or brunch of smashed avo with poached eggs – then end on a sweet high with a homemade cocoa nib brownie.

ESTABLISHED
2012

KEY ROASTER
Crankhouse Coffee

BREWING METHOD
Espresso, V60, AeroPress, Moccamaster, nitro cold brew

MACHINE
La Marzocco Linea Classic

GRINDER
Mahlkonig, Anfim

OPENING HOURS
Mon-Fri 8am-5.30pm
Sat 8.30am-6pm
Sun 10am-4pm

 Gluten FREE

 BEANS AVAILABLE INSTORE

 OUTDOOR SEATING

 BRING YOUR OWN *Cup*

T: 07507 724498

f @devoncoffeeexeter   🐦 @devoncoffee88   📷 @devoncoffeeexeter

81 MARCH COFFEE

87 South Street, Exeter, Devon, EX1 1EQ

The March team had such passion for top-notch coffee and home-cooked food that they were driven to share their fervour with their fellow caffeine fans in the city. And once they'd added a warm-and-bright-but-oh-so-cool interior, the draw was irresistible.

Local roastery Crankhouse provides the house coffee (ably assisted by Caravan), and drinks are delivered via the La Marzocco Strada or Wilfa batch brew. Espresso grinding duty falls to an EK43 which, coupled with the Strada, delivers reliably clean and sweet shots.

TIP RHUBARB CREAM, FUDGE OR MATCHA DOUGHNUT? TAKE YOUR PICK OF THE BUNCH

Coffee may be the centre of March's universe, but the food certainly ain't shabby. Tempting bakes – all attentively made in-house – crowd the counter, and the indulgent doughnuts overflowing with imaginative fillings have gained a cult following.

Lazy weekends are welcomed in with a Friday-to-Sunday brunch menu. Vegans are treated to coconut soy mushrooms or smashed avo, while carnivores can't go wrong with brioche french toast with bacon and maple syrup. During the working week, the busy folk of Exeter are fuelled by March's epic sourdough doorstop sarnies.

ESTABLISHED
2017

KEY ROASTER
Crankhouse Coffee

BREWING METHOD
Espresso, batch brew

MACHINE
La Marzocco Strada

GRINDER
Mahlkonig EK43

OPENING HOURS
Mon-Fri 8.30am-4.30pm
Sat 9am-5.30pm
Sun 10am-4pm

Gluten FREE

BEANS AVAILABLE

INSTORE

WIFI

---

www.marchcoffee.co.uk   T: 07972 694606

f @marchcoffeeexeter   🐦 @marchcoffeeexe   📷 @marchcoffeeexeter

MAP № 82 CALYPSO COFFEE COMPANY

45 Fleet Street, Torquay, Devon, TQ2 5DW

Spilling out onto Torquay's bustling Fleet Street, the aroma of Calypso's artisan coffee is an irresistible draw for passing shoppers and on-a-mission workers.

Perch at a cable-drum table outside and watch 'em succumb to the heavenly scent as you relax with a filter coffee, expertly hand-brewed via Chemex, AeroPress or V60 kit.

Espresso comes courtesy of the La Marzocco and can be pimped to make some of Calypso's idiosyncratic signature coffees. Purists may sniff at pistachio or lavender cream options, but the adventurous can't get enough of the Colonna single origin beans which form the base of all the brews.

INSIDER'S TIP
THE BEST-SELLING BAILEYS FLAT WHITE IS WHERE COFFEE BREAK MEETS COCKTAIL HOUR

Homemade speciality bagels stuffed with off-the-chart delicious fillings make very happy bedfellows for the coffee. A sweet breakfast number matched with a smooth pourover will kickstart even the dullest of mornings or, if you're feeling virtuous, a superfood smoothie will treat your body like a temple.

ESTABLISHED
2015

KEY ROASTER
Colonna Coffee

BREWING METHOD
Espresso, V60, drip, cold brew, Chemex, AeroPress

MACHINE
La Marzocco Linea 3AV

GRINDER
Mazzer Kony, Mahlkonig Tanzania, Baratza Sette

OPENING HOURS
Mon-Sat 8.30am-6.30pm
Sun 9am-6pm
(extended in summer)

Gluten FREE

BEANS AVAILABLE
INSTORE

WIFI

CYCLE FRIENDLY

OUTDOOR Seating

FAMILY FRIENDLY

DISABLED ACCESS

BRING YOUR OWN Cup

COFFEE COURSES ►

T: 01803 213728

f @calypsotorquay ◎ @calypso_coffee

MAP № 83 PORT ESPRESSO

26 Middle Street, Brixham, Devon, TQ5 8ER

As the boats clank and seagulls screech in the harbour, canny Brixham locals retire to the welcoming embrace of Port Espresso.

Eclectic interiors invite you to take a load off – either people watching from the sunny window or snuggled up out back where you can nurse your coffee in seclusion.

The house roast is taken very seriously: it's served double ristretto (where natural sweetness collides with richly caffeinated notes) as standard. Gentler flat whites (with the perfect amount of steamed milk) are also a fave here.

INSIDER'S TIP GET THE PORT ESPRESSO PLAYLIST ON SPOTIFY TO RECREATE THE EXPERIENCE AT HOME

When breakfast's a distant memory and it feels like an awfully long time until lunch, grab a Port Espresso brunch. Sister shop and craft bakery 5 Doors Up provides the sourdough which forms the centrepiece of many an egg-based dish here. Alternatively, opt for french toast with caramelised banana if you believe there should be more pudding opps in a single day.

On Sunday mornings, roll along to the Breakfast Club and quietly revel in comfort food and wake-me-gently vibes.

ESTABLISHED
2016

KEY ROASTER
Voyager Coffee

BREWING METHOD
Espresso, V60

MACHINE
La Spaziale S5

GRINDER
Anfim

OPENING HOURS
Mon-Sat 7am-4pm
Sun 8am-12pm

Gluten FREE

BEANS AVAILABLE
INSTORE

WIFI

OUTDOOR SEATING

BRING YOUR OWN Cup.

COFFEE COURSES

---

www.portespresso.co   T: 01803 411120

f @portespresso   ⊙ @portespresso

MAP 84 MOOR AT 13

13 Fore Street, Kingswear, Devon, TQ6 0AD

Sharpen your elbows ahead of a trip to this south Devon fresher as, should you spy the window seat free, you'll be budging coffee folk out of the way for first dibs on the spot.

The coveted table within the industrial-chic cafe has one of the best views in Kingsbridge of the River Dart below.

Order a cup of the Roastworks coffee, pair it with a banana and pineapple muffin with cream cheese frosting, and you could easily lose a couple of hours watching the boats bob by.

TIP BRING YOUR POOCH – MOOR IS SUPER PUP FRIENDLY

Owners Lottie Fern and Jamie Fenton only opened the sociable space in spring 2018 but they've already earned Moor a reputation for its speciality of scrambled eggs. Made with organic free-range eggs from a farm up the hill, the sky-high stack is the perfect comfort food fix.

Once you've had your fill of quality caffeine and homemade grub, stock up on local preserves, biscuits and coffee beans at the in-house deli.

ESTABLISHED
2018

KEY ROASTER
Roastworks
Coffee Co.

BREWING METHOD
Espresso

MACHINE
La Spaziale S5
Compact

GRINDER
Mahlkonig K30
Vario

OPENING HOURS
Thu-Tue 7am-4pm

T: 01803 752225
f @moorat13 @moor13devon

MAP № 85 ALMOND THIEF BAKERY

Unit 3-4, Webber's Yard, Dartington, Devon, TQ9 6JY

Good luck staying on the wagon when you swing by this Dartington coffee stop, as its counter of freshly baked beauties has been the downfall of many a calorie-counting wellness-warrior.

Almond Thief favourites such as the irresistibly gooey chocolate cookies make an exceptional match for expertly prepared coffee. Or plump for a pastel de nata – surely the best outside of Portugal? – which pairs perfectly with silky espresso.

The coffee in question is kept interesting by a lively line-up of roasting greats – previous appearances have included Yallah, Crankhouse and Voyager.

TIP INSIDER'S SUCKER FOR A BAKERY HYBRID? TRY THE CUSTARD FILLED CINNAMON SWIRL

It's not all greed and sweet gluttony though, as the busy kitchen also cranks out a colourful bill of homemade breakfast, brunch and lunch dishes. Whatever you go for (tip: the Turkish eggs are particularly good), make sure to order a side of the superb sourdough which is made using grain grown less than a mile away.

In a rush? Have a loaf wrapped to-go and take the bakery vibe home.

ESTABLISHED
2015

KEY ROASTER
Multiple roasters

BREWING METHOD
Espresso

MACHINE
La Marzocco Linea PB

GRINDER
Mythos One Clima Pro

OPENING HOURS
Tue-Fri 8am-3pm
Sat 9am-3pm

Gluten FREE

BEANS AVAILABLE INSTORE

WIFI

CYCLE FRIENDLY

OUTDOOR seating

FAMILY FRIENDLY

DISABLED ACCESS

BRING YOUR OWN cup.

www.thealmondthief.com   T: 01803 411290

f @thealmondthief   🐦 @thealmondthief   📷 @thealmondthief

MAP № 86 THE LEAPING SALMON

Horrabridge, Yelverton, Devon, PL20 7TN

A riverside cafe within a rural village pub, this unassuming gem is a far cry from the consciously cool coffee hangouts of Bristol and beyond – and all the more of a find for it.

Owners Max Phillips and Fred Andrews took over in 2017 and spent almost a year renovating the inn and transforming its second bar into a cafe. *'It's great to offer speciality somewhere you wouldn't normally expect to find it,'* says Max. *'And it complements everything else we are doing.'*

INSIDER TIP THERE ARE THREE CHARMING GUEST ROOMS UPSTAIRS IF YOU'RE ROAD TRIPPING ACROSS THE SOUTH WEST

While the Square Mile espresso and guest roast batch brew add a dash of metropolitan Melbourne to this pocket of rural Devon, homemade saffron buns, hot-from-the-oven pasties and rhubarb bakewell slices are in keeping with The Leaping Salmon's sleepy Dartmoor setting.

Stick around for lunch or supper at the pub next door (you've made the journey after all) and feast on crowd-pleasers crafted from garden-grown veggies, homemade sourdough and locally reared produce.

ESTABLISHED
2018

KEY ROASTER
Square Mile
Coffee Roasters

BREWING METHOD
Espresso,
batch filter

MACHINE
La Marzocco,
Moccamaster

GRINDER
Mahlkonig K30

OPENING HOURS
Tue-Sat 9am-11pm
Sun 12pm-11pm

 Gluten FREE

 BEANS AVAILABLE / INSTORE

 WIFI

CYCLE FRIENDLY

 OUTDOOR seating

 FAMILY FRIENDLY

 DISABLED ACCESS

 BRING YOUR OWN Cup

www.theleapingsalmon.co.uk   T: 01822 851541
f @theleapingsalmonpub   @theleapingsalmon

MAP № 87 HANGRY

68 Ebrington Street, Plymouth, Devon, PL4 9AQ

Like Clark Kent, Hangry has two guises. By day it's a Shoreditch-meets-Brooklyn brunch spot that serves dishes across the spectrum – from meaty to vegan – alongside standout coffee. At night, the shakers are unleashed and out come the cocktails (and craft beers).

To experience the thrills, head to Ebrington Street, just off Plymouth's waterfront, where the coffee goes down amid buzzy vibes and vibrant colour-pop decor.

Supporting local and small suppliers is central to its ethos, so Exeter's Crankhouse is the hero roastery here with guest appearances from other regional roasters. The coffee prep isn't showy either and simple espresso, filter and V60 let the quality of the beans and the roast do the talking.

TIP 10 PER CENT IS KNOCKED OFF THE PRICE OF YOUR COFFEE IF YOU TAKE A REUSABLE CUP

Americana infiltrates the all-day menu, with fried chicken and waffles served with burnt sweetcorn succotash and maple dressing providing a taste of the deep south. Veggies and vegans aren't left out of the party – there are plenty of drool-worthy dishes to choose from and inventive ways to convert meaty options.

ESTABLISHED
2018

KEY ROASTER
Crankhouse Coffee

BREWING METHOD
Espresso, V60, filter

MACHINE
Gaggia D90

GRINDER
Fiorenzato F64

OPENING HOURS
Tue-Thu 9am-5pm
Fri 9am-9pm
Sat 10am-9pm
Sun 10am-4pm

---

www.hangryrestaurants.co.uk   T: 01752 262618

f @hangryplymouth   @hangry_plymouth

ᴹᴬᴾ 88 BOSTON TEA PARTY – PLYMOUTH

Jamaica House, 82-84 Vauxhall Street, Sutton Harbour, Plymouth, Devon, PL4 0EX

I n true Boston Tea Party style, the Plymouth outpost resides in a beautiful Grade II-listed building that oozes with history.

The Jamaica House cafe is one of the heftier members of the BTP family and has space for 150 caffeine chuggers and cake cravers to get their fill while taking in the views over Sutton Harbour.

Upcycled furniture and fittings, old gymnasium flooring and refashioned school chairs give the urban hangout its unique charm and create a fun and funky space where visitors can catch up with friends over a flat white or get down to work after a kickstarter of sunny-side-up eggs.

TIP DON'T FORGET YOUR REUSABLE: BOSTON BANNED SINGLE-USE CUPS IN MAY 2018

The BTP house blend, which is crafted by the beansmiths at Extract, has been refined and reworked over the past seven years in the pursuit of sensationally smooth espresso. Lavished with gently steamed milk it's all malt, biscuit and chocolate deliciousness. Go black and it's a cocoa, black cherry and honeycomb story.

ESTABLISHED
2015

KEY ROASTER
Extract Coffee Roasters

BREWING METHOD
Espresso, filter

MACHINE
La Marzocco Linea PB

GRINDER
Mythos One, Mazzer Major

OPENING HOURS
Mon-Sat 7am-7pm
Sun 8am-7pm

www.bostonteaparty.co.uk   T: 01752 267862
f @btpcafes   🐦 @btpcafes   📷 @btpcafes

MAP 89 ROCKETS & RASCALS

7 Parade, The Barbican, Plymouth, Devon, PL1 2JL

Plymouth's cycle-centric speciality hangout received a refresh this year, which means even more space for its lycra-clad followers to refuel before hitting the saddle.

Two-wheeled revellers aren't the only folk scheduling a pit stop at this Barbican cafe, however. You'll also find caffeine enthusiasts rubbing shoulders with tourists as they congregate here in search of a cup of the good stuff.

Neighbours The Devon Coffee Company stock the grinder and keep the retail shelves filled with banging beans which have been roasted just a short bike ride away. Try the traditional Seadog blend on espresso or a single origin Aviator as batch brew.

TIP FEELING THE CHILL? TRY ONE OF AMBER'S WINTER WARMING SOUPS

Cross-country pursuits are sustained with sourdough toasties (word is that the spreadable chorizo on toast is worth making a pig of yourself over) followed by a slab of something sweet from nearby Cobbles Bakery.

If you can, plan a trip to coincide with the live music on Friday nights or weekend cycle events.

ESTABLISHED
2013

KEY ROASTER
The Devon
Coffee Company

BREWING METHOD
Espresso,
batch brew

MACHINE
Astoria Perla
Lever

GRINDER
Fiorenzato F64
EVO, Ceado
E37S, Fiorenzato
F6, Compak K3

OPENING HOURS
Mon-Sat 8am-6pm
Sun 9am-5pm

www.rockettrading.co.uk   T: 01752 927555
f @rocketsandrascals @rocketsnrascals @rockettradingco

ALL THE TASTE, NONE OF THE LACTOSE

Lactofree is the best alternative to standard milk for creating a latte that is easier to digest*.

Enjoy the great taste of a real dairy latte, just without the lactose.

*Easier to digest for those who may have gastro-intestinal discomfort caused by lactose intake.

DELICIOUS LATTE MADE WITH ARLA LACTOFREE

Arla
lactofree

SEMI SKIMMED
LACTOSE FREE*
DAIRY DRINK

№ 90 THE HUTONG CAFE

160 Cremyll Street, Stonehouse, Plymouth, Devon, PL1 3RB

Step from the busy harbourside into the rustic-chic surroundings of The Hutong Cafe for a coffee experience that's as dynamic as it is assured.

Making a damn fine cup of coffee is The Hutong's mission, and alongside its love of the bean is a passion to share the craft. The team want to guide customers through the subtleties of bean varieties, roast profiles and brew, and are committed to raising speciality's profile in Plymouth.

Roastworks is the roastery in residence but is kept company by a revolving roster of guests which includes Dark Arts, Ozone and Small Batch. Drinks are delivered via espresso, batch brew or drip methods, with The Hutong's flat white proving a popular standout. Syrups concocted from super-sweet jaggery and rapadura are in development to add an extra shot of exotic oomph to your cup.

TIP HUTONG'S LINE-UP OF EVENTS ATTRACTS A LIVELY LOCAL FOLLOWING

The seasonal food menu is refined while remaining substantial and, alongside cultural events like comedy evenings and coffee night markets, is another draw for punters from nearby Royal William Yard.

ESTABLISHED
2018

KEY ROASTER
Roastworks
Coffee Co.

BREWING METHOD
Espresso, drip,
batch brew,

MACHINE
Nuova Simonelli
Premier Maxi 2

GRINDER
Mahlkonig K30
Air

OPENING HOURS
Mon, Wed-Thu
7.30am-**5**pm
Fri **7.30**am-**4**pm
Sat-Sun **8**am-**4**pm

Gluten FREE

BEANS AVAILABLE INSTORE

WIFI

OUTDOOR seating

FAMILY FRiENDLY

DISABLED ACCESS

BRING YOUR OWN Cup

COFFEE COURSES

T: 07455 376377

f @thehutongcafe @thehutongcafe @thehutongcafe

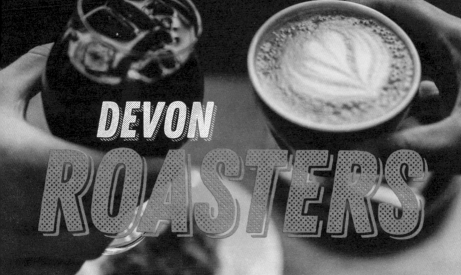

DEVON
ROASTERS

MAP No 91 ROASTWORKS COFFEE CO.

Unit 7, Blackdown Park, Willand, Devon, EX15 2FS

'*Speciality coffee needs to be way more inclusive and to achieve this we need to engage with customers. How are we doing this? Kickass products and a kickass brand.*' Fighting talk, indeed, from Roastworks' founder Will Little.

For the Devon roastery crew, 2018 was all about punching their way out of their 'micro roaster' weight category and establishing themselves as a serious speciality heavyweight.

ESTABLISHED
2014

ROASTER
MAKE & SIZE
G.W. Barth
Menado 60kg
Probat LG12

OPEN
BY APPOINTMENT

BEANS
AVAILABLE
ONLINE

'ROASTWORKS' NESPRESSO-COMPATIBLE CAPSULES ARE 100 PER CENT RECYCLABLE'

To win over discerning coffee folk, the growing team have supplemented their house blend (crafted from ethically sourced beans roasted on a 60kg vintage drum roaster) with a winning bill of additional coffees – both single origins and blends.

Roastworks' commitment to making speciality coffee less of an elite sport is matched by its determination to positively influence the industry through innovation. This year the team also launched their Nespresso-compatible capsules which are 100 per cent recyclable.

www.roastworks.co.uk   T: 01884 829400

f @roastworkscoffeeco   @roastworksdevon   @roastworks_coffee_co

MAP № 92 COFFEE FACTORY

Unit 3, Seaton Junction, Axminster, Devon, EX13 7PW

Inspired by a trip down under, Justine and Danny Parfitt were determined to share their love of a well-crafted cup when back home in the UK. So much so that they opened a coffee bar. Then, unable to find the perfect roastery to stock their grinders, the pair took another leap and started roasting their own.

After several years honing their small batch roasting skills, they acquired a 1950s vintage Probat (known as Dorothy) which, after a bit of love and attention – and a few techy adaptations – now takes centre stage at the Coffee Factory's Axminster roastery.

ESTABLISHED
2009

ROASTER
MAKE & SIZE
Vintage Probat
UG 22kg

'THE ETHIOPIAN ARICHA-EDIDO SCOOPED A 2018 THREE STAR GREAT TASTE AWARD'

The pair's mission to provide ethically sourced coffee to people's homes and businesses has yielded an impressive subscription service. From smooth, nutty blends to sensational single origins, there's something to keep every kind of caffeine addict buzzing. The Roasters Choice™ subscription, which includes the team's favourite picks from the cupping table, is particularly popular.

Pop by to see Dorothy in action and sample some freshly roasted, ground and brewed coffee for yourself.

www.thecoffeefactory.co.uk T: 01297 551259
f @coffeefactorydevon @coffee_factory @coffee_factory

MAP 93 CRANKHOUSE COFFEE

Great Matridge, Longdown, Exeter, Devon, EX6 7BE

There's a reason why so many of the South West's discerning speciality cafe owners worship at the Crankhouse temple: they recognise that founder Dave Stanton has an inspired touch, fuelled by single-minded zeal – and a drop or two of his own espresso.

From this depths-of-Devon roastery, a rotating house blend is perfected alongside a palate-thrilling array of single origins. The aim is to put speciality coffee within the grasp of every wo/man on the street – and Dave's enthusiasm for the task is infectious.

'SOAK UP SOME OF DAVE'S LIMITLESS CAFFEINE KNOWLEDGE AT ONE OF THE EXETER CUPPING SESSIONS'

Meticulous sourcing through ethical and sustainable importers sees peachy florals from Ethiopia rub shoulders with choc-and-nut Brazilian intensity. Exclusive micro lots are regularly on offer to those quick enough to sniff them out, and a recent recce around Costa Rica has yielded a number of direct-trade coffees for the caffeine connoisseur.

To soak up some of Dave's limitless caffeine knowledge, and develop your sensory skills, drop in on one of Crankhouse's weekly Exeter cupping sessions.

ESTABLISHED
2014

ROASTER
MAKE & SIZE
Petroncini TT7.5

OPEN
BY APPOINTMENT

COFFEE
COURSES

BEANS
AVAILABLE
ONLINE DINESITE

www.crankhousecoffee.co.uk   T: 07588 020288

f @crankhousecoffee   @crankhouseroast   @crankhouseroast

Don't be bland

For freakin' delicious marketing, creative design and publishing from
experts in food, drink and hospitality, just add salt

01271 859299 | saltmedia.co.uk

salt media

MAP 94 THE DEVON COFFEE COMPANY

195 Faraday Mill, Plymouth, Devon, PL4 0ST

Two years on from moving into their new roastery, The Devon Coffee Company is flourishing. The training school, which provides baristas with an in-depth understanding of the dark arts of coffee extraction and preparation, is being expanded into a SCA-accredited training campus.

'This will provide a facility jam-packed with all the equipment and knowledge a barista requires to hone their skills and receive industry recognised certification,' explains owner Andrew Baker.

Baristas across the South West can be confident that they're pulling the sweetest shots, as the team's freshly roasted seasonal espresso blends (Gumdrop, Super Eight and The Americas) and single origins come with full technical support and training.

'THE WHITE LABEL SERVICE OFFERS FULL CONTROL'

Cafes looking for something unique can take advantage of the bespoke white label service which offers them full control over their coffee – everything from the choice of green beans through to the roasting style and branding.

Domestic dabblers, meanwhile, can enjoy the delights of The Devon Coffee Club subscription.

ESTABLISHED
2011

ROASTER
MAKE & SIZE
Besca 15kg
North 1kg

OPEN
BY APPOINTMENT

COFFEE
COURSES

COURSES

BEANS
AVAILABLE

ONLINE

www.devoncoffeecompany.com   T: 01752 222567
f @devoncoffeecompany   @devoncoffeeco   @devoncoffeecompany

CORNWALL

Nº100
YALLAH COFFEE KIOSK

coffee

DOUGH·NUTS

YALLAH
COFFEE ROASTERS

DONUTS

Stone clean, fresh doughnuts
made by St Ives Bakery.

Jam	2.0
Sugar Coated	2.0
Custard	2.5
Daily Special	2.5

COFFEE BAGS

250 G	8
1 KG	28

HOT CHOCOLATE TINS

250 G	10

KEEP CUPS

Small	15
Large	20

This Kiosk is single use plastic
free. All of our products have
bio-degradable or recycled
packaging.

We believe our suppliers are
some of the best in the country.
They care about the quality of
their products, the ingredients
they use and the footprint of
their company.

Thanks for stopping by.

@YALLAHCOFFEE
YALLAHCOFFEE.CO.UK

CAFE

95 Temple
96 North Coast Wine Co
97 Woods Cafe
98 Strong Adolfos
99 Gylly Beach Cafe
100 Yallah Coffee Kiosk
101 The Yellow Canary Cafe

ROASTER

102 Sabins Small Batch Roasters
103 Yallah Coffee

*All locations are approximate

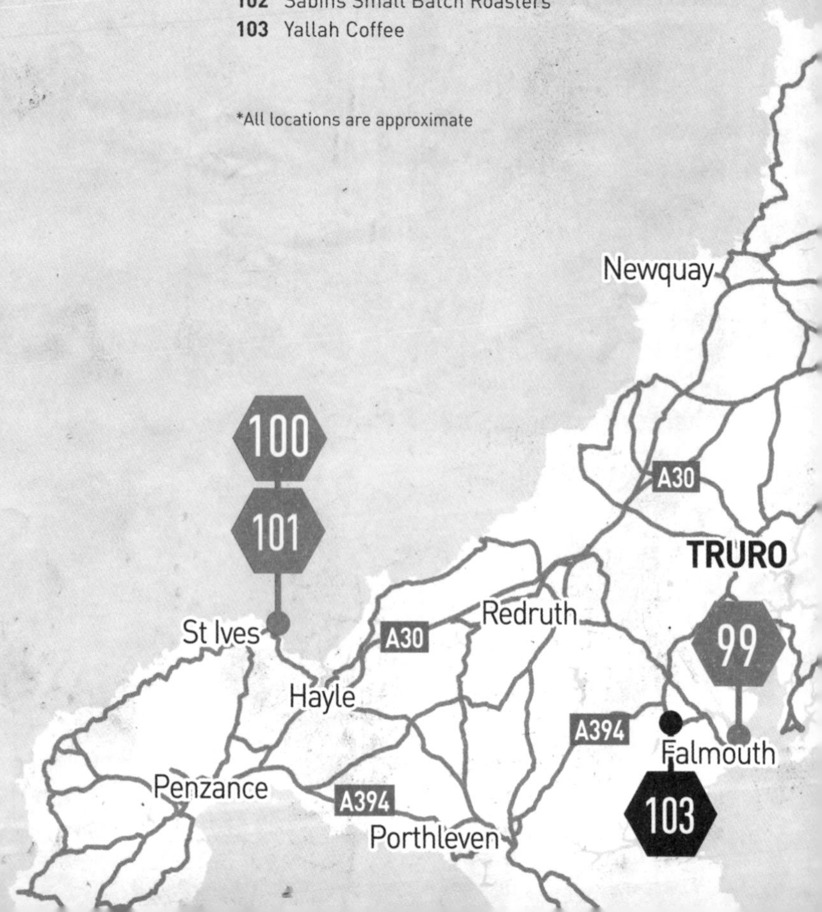
Newquay
100
101
A30
TRURO
Redruth
St Ives
A30
99
Hayle
A394
Falmouth
Penzance
A394
103
Porthleven

MAP No 95 TEMPLE

10 Granville Terrace, Bude, Cornwall, EX23 8JZ

B ude's innovative new temple to clean eating, culture and coffee only opened in December 2017, but the vibrant venue has already built a loyal following.

The calming oasis of food, fashion and evening feasts showcases a progressive menu of gorgeous organic dishes alongside the house fave: a grilled sarnie made with Coombeshead Farm sourdough, Cornish cheddar and homemade kimchi.

INSIDERS TIP CHECK OUT THE LIFESTYLE, HOMEWARE AND CLOTHING STORE

However, it's the appearance of Allpress beans that seduces speciality worshippers and encourages them to linger over the line-up of espresso-based drinks.

The Temple team are out to challenge the food and drink chain by working with small, sustainable suppliers, as well as being on a mission to create healthy dishes which taste incredible.

Laid-back and light-filled by day, at night the spot morphs into a chilled out restaurant which makes the most of impeccably sourced Cornish ingredients and organic wines.

ESTABLISHED
2017

KEY ROASTER
Allpress
Espresso

BREWING METHOD
Espresso

MACHINE
La Marzocco

GRINDER
Mazzer Luigi

OPENING HOURS
Tue-Sat
10am-4pm, 6pm-11pm
Sun 10am-4pm

 Gluten FREE

 BEANS AVAILABLE INSTORE

 WIFI

 CYCLE FRIENDLY

 OUTDOOR seating

 FAMILY FRIENDLY

 BRING YOUR OWN Cup.

www.templecornwall.com   T: 01288 354739

f @templecornwall   @ @templebude

MAP 96 NORTH COAST WINE CO

1 Lansdown Road, Bude, Cornwall, EX23 8BH

This wine merchant, cocktail bar and cafe rolled into one features such an eclectic list of wines, spirits and craft beers, that it would be a crime not to browse while sipping your preferred brew – be it a flat white or single origin chocolate mocha.

The Bude-based bolthole is the pit stop of choice for explorers fresh from Cornwall's coastline: day trippers, seasoned surfers and long weekenders alike swing by for a hit of quality caffeine and/or a cheeky lunchtime tipple.

Designated driver? North Coast Wine Co has it covered, as barista and mixologist Chris Ryder knocks up a cracking coffee tonic. Made with the stonking own-brewed cold brew, it's a unique and refreshing fix before hitting the A39.

TIP CHECK OUT THE 600-STRONG WINE COLLECTION AND LENGTHY LIST OF LOCAL CRAFT BEERS

On the coffee front, Monsoon Estate's Papua New Guinea Enorga delivers chocolatey flavours and hug-in-a-mug warmth and authenticity.

A varied selection of Stratford-upon-Avon roasted beans are also available to take home – ask the team and they'll happily grind the latest batch to suit your preferred home brewing style. Alternatively, sip in store and soak up the cafe vibes from one of the 1920s cinema chairs.

ESTABLISHED
2016

KEY ROASTER
Monsoon Estates Coffee Company

BREWING METHOD
Espresso, cold brew

MACHINE
La Spaziale S5

GRINDER
Mahlkonig K30 Vario Air

OPENING HOURS
Mon-Thu 10am-6pm
Fri-Sat 10am-9pm

 BEANS AVAILABLE INSTORE

 WIFI

 CYCLE FRIENDLY

 OUTDOOR seating

 FAMILY FRIENDLY

 DISABLED ACCESS

 BRING YOUR OWN Cup

www.ncwine.co.uk   T: 01288 354304

f @northcoastwineco   🐦 @ncwine1   📷 @northcoastwineco

MAP№ 97 WOODS CAFE

Callywith Cottage, Cardinham Woods, Bodmin, Cornwall, PL30 4AL

In a steep-sided valley on the edge of Cardinham Woods, a little stone cottage sits with smoke wisping from the chimney, its homely exterior beckoning wanderers in.

So far, so Hansel and Gretel. If, that is, Hansel and Gretel were into speciality coffee with a stonkingly good scone on the side.

Yallah's fairly traded, single origin beans travel up the A30 from Falmouth to be carefully extracted via Woods' La Marzocco machine, while co-owner Lara Spurrell gets to work on the mountain of fluffy scones which are scoffed at the cosy cottage each day.

TIP TOP-NOTCH COFFEE IS MATCHED BY CORNISH-GROWN TEA BLENDS

Doorstop sarnies make the most of local goodies like Cornish brie and Davidstow cheddar, and vie for attention alongside tempting bakes which are also made in the cafe's busy kitchen.

Follow a yomp in the woods with a sizeable slab of Victoria sponge and a flat white in the clearing-in-the-woods garden (or beside the log burner if the weather's taken a turn) for a fairytale ending to your day.

ESTABLISHED
2009

KEY ROASTER
Yallah Coffee

BREWING METHOD
Espresso

MACHINE
La Marzocco

GRINDER
Compak

OPENING HOURS
Mon-Sun 10am-4.30pm
(extended in summer)

---

www.woodscafe.co.uk   T: 01208 78111

f @woodscafecornwall   🐦 @woodscafekernow   📷 @woodscafe

MAP 98 STRONG ADOLFOS

Hawksfield, A39, Wadebridge, Cornwall, PL27 7LR

Surf, cycle and coffee cultures collide at this roadside hangout where bikers swing by on vintage choppers, colourful boards adorn the walls and baristas pull Cornish espresso.

The unlikely spot on the A39 near Wadebridge doesn't simply draw in surfers fresh from the waves and coffee fans heading through Cornwall; with its killer kitchen team crafting brunch, lunch and epic bakes from scratch, it's also become a favourite with holidaymakers and locals willing to make a short detour.

TIP DESIGNATED BACK SEAT DRIVER? CHECK OUT THE LINE-UP OF LOCAL CRAFT BEERS

While the Origin coffee restores weary drivers, and locally-sourced breakfasts fuel the whole family for onward travels, the cakes are a non-essential not to be missed. Inspired by the Scandi custom of fika, Swedish co-owner Mathilda oversees an incredible line-up of delights including cardamom buns and drömmar cookies.

Caffeinated and ready for the road, don't leave without stocking up on Cornish produce, wines and spirits at The Arc food store next door.

ESTABLISHED
2013

KEY ROASTER
Origin Coffee Roasters

BREWING METHOD
Espresso, filter

MACHINE
La Marzocco Linea PB

GRINDER
Nuova Simonelli Mythos One

OPENING HOURS
Mon-Fri 8.30am-4pm
Sat-Sun 9am-4pm

 Gluten FREE

 BEANS AVAILABLE INSTORE

 WIFI

 CYCLE FRIENDLY

 OUTDOOR seating

 FAMILY FRIENDLY

 DISABLED ACCESS

 BRING YOUR OWN cup

 COFFEE COURSES

---

www.strongadolfos.com T: 01208 816949

f @strongadolfos 🐦 @strongadolfos 📷 @strongadolfos

MAP 99 GYLLY BEACH CAFE

On Gyllyngvase Beach, Cliff Road, Falmouth, Cornwall, TR11 4PA

Fancy sipping espresso to the soundtrack of swirling seas, squawking seagulls and kids squealing in the waves? For a speciality-on-sea experience, Gylly Beach Cafe is hard to beat.

Beans roasted by Origin taste even bolder and sweeter against the backdrop of a beautiful beach with awesome views across to the Lizard Peninsula and Helford River.

Sand loafers compete for a seat on the sunny terrace for their brekkie of baked waffles, while those riding the South West swell head back to shore for a midday snack of seasonal seafood. But it's in the evening that the beachside banquet really begins. Cornish delicacies such as Primrose Herd pig cheek and monkfish wellington are prepared with flair by *Masterchef: The Professionals* quarter finalist, Dale McIntosh.

TIP ENJOY FLAMING FISHY FEASTS AT THE WEEKEND BEACH BARBECUES

Don't miss the daily changing muffins, cakes, brownies and bread fresh from Gylly's own bakery next door – perfect with a decaf San Fermin americano on the sand.

ESTABLISHED
2000

KEY ROASTER
Origin Coffee Roasters

BREWING METHOD
Espresso

MACHINE
La Marzocco

GRINDER
Expresso Italiano

OPENING HOURS
Mon-Sat 9am-late

Gluten FREE

CYCLE FRIENDLY

OUTDOOR seating

FAMILY FRIENDLY

DISABLED ACCESS

BRING YOUR OWN cup

---

www.gyllybeach.com   T: 01326 312884

f @gyllybeachcafe   🐦 @gyllybeachcafe   📷 @gyllybeachcafe

MAP № 100 YALLAH COFFEE KIOSK

Court Arcade, Wharf Road, St Ives, Cornwall, TR26 1LF

A seaside hatch is an unlikely place to find incredible caffeine, yet Yallah founder Rich Blake is changing the speciality game in surfy St Ives. After all, why should you have to settle for rubbish coffee when you're drinking in some of Cornwall's best views?

It may be slight in size, but mighty flavours emerge from the Kiosk. The espresso, made with freshly ground beans and extracted on a Sanremo Cafe Racer, cycles through Yallah's Explore range. That means thought-provoking flavours and experimental profiles that'll blow your preconceptions about hole-in-the-wall coffee out of the water.

INSIDER'S TIP EXPAND YOUR SPECIALITY SKILLSET AT ONE OF YALLAH'S SATURDAY COFFEE COURSES

Coffee is the main event here, but fresh doughnuts from the St Ives Bakery make the perfect chaser. In keeping with Yallah's high standards of sustainability, single-use plastics are frowned upon and all packaging is biodegradable or recycled and reusable cups are available. Non-homogenised milk travels all of four miles from Trink Dairy's grass-fed herd, and non-dairy alternatives are available for plant-based latte lovers.

ESTABLISHED
2018

KEY ROASTER
Yallah Coffee

BREWING METHOD
Espresso

MACHINE
Sanremo Cafe Racer

GRINDER
Mythos One Clima Pro, Mahlkonig EK43

OPENING HOURS
Mon-Sun 8am-4pm

BEANS AVAILABLE INSTORE

WIFI

CYCLE FRIENDLY

FAMILY FRIENDLY

BRING YOUR OWN Cup

COFFEE COURSES

---

www.yallahcoffee.co.uk   T: 01326 72783

f @yallahcoffee   🐦 @yallahcoffee   📷 @yallahcoffee

MAP 101 THE YELLOW CANARY CAFE

12 Fore Street, St Ives, Cornwall, TR26 1AB

amid the bustle of Fore Street, and surrounded by gift shops and boutiques, you'll find something of a St Ives institution.

The Yellow Canary Cafe has stood its ground for over 45 years, continuously building its reputation for good food and quality coffee.

INSIDER'S TIP AT HIGH TIDE GRAB A STEAMING FLAT WHITE TO ENJOY ON SMEATONS PIER AS WAVES CRASH AROUND YOU

As you stroll past the cafe and towards the sea, the window (chocka with traditional pasties and cakes) is alluring, but it's the waft of Origin coffee pulled through the La Marzocco that's the real seducer.

Directly traded beans are delivered via drip or as espresso and, with over four decades of practice, The Canary's adept at making a decent brew. Daily-changing roasts are chalked up on the board, along with the date of roasting, so you can keep up to speed with what's on.

Sarnies hewn from artisan bread satisfy sea-air appetites: keep it local with crab served with lemon mayo. Vegans and gluten-avoiders won't be disappointed either as there are plenty of free-from options.

ESTABLISHED
1972

KEY ROASTER
Origin Coffee Roasters

BREWING METHOD
Espresso, drip

MACHINE
La Marzocco Linea PB

GRINDER
Mazzer Major E

OPENING HOURS
Mon-Sun 9am-5pm
(extended in summer)

T: 01736 797118

 @theyellowcanarycafe @theyellowcanarycafe

CORNWALL ROASTERS

MAP 102 SABINS SMALL BATCH ROASTERS

Butterfly Barn, Hersham, Bude, Cornwall, EX23 9LZ

Visitors to this bijou roastery tend to be bowled over by the bucolic setting – an adorable shed tucked away on a smallholding in a secluded Cornish hamlet.

It's even more charming when you're warmly welcomed by the free-spirited family behind this small batch roastery: Paul and Emma Sabin and their six home-schooled children.

Their two back garden beauties – a pair of Topers – are fired up five days a week to roast the seasonal micro lots. *'We're always on the lookout for the unusual and the unique and get to sample the most amazing beans,'* says Emma. *'It's interesting and creative – and we get to take people on an adventure with us.'*

ESTABLISHED
2014

ROASTER
MAKE & SIZE
Toper x 2

OPEN
BY APPOINTMENT

COFFEE
COURSES

BEANS
AVAILABLE
ONLINE | ONSITE

'SABINS SUPPORT TWO CHILDREN THROUGH THE SOS AFRICA CHARITY COFFEE PROGRAMME'

Exciting developments this year include eldest daughter Florence enrolling as a full-time apprentice, the introduction of a collection scheme where local customers' grounds are recycled into coffee logs and a Comoros conservation coffee to help endangered bats.

The family also continue to support two South African children through the SOS Africa charity coffee programme.

www.sabinscoffee.co.uk   T: 01288 321660
f @sabinscoffee   @sabinscoffee   @sabins_coffee

MAP № 103 YALLAH COFFEE

Argal Home Farm, Kergilliack, Falmouth, Cornwall, TR11 5PD

Yallah's manifesto is simple: top-notch coffee which is honestly produced without pretension. Founder Richard Blake wants us to think about the coffee we drink in a way which doesn't make our heads hurt.

His philosophy is the reason that the Cornish roastery is a strictly single origin set-up and only sources beans which are directly traded from the most sustainable farms. The whole Yallah operation is hands-on (including roaster restoration and packaging design) to ensure quality and fairness at every step.

ESTABLISHED
2014

ROASTER
MAKE & SIZE
Virey Garnier 15kg
Otto Swadlo 3kg

OPEN
BY APPOINTMENT

COFFEE
COURSES

BEANS
AVAILABLE
ONLINE OFFSITE

'FOUNDER RICHARD BLAKE WANTS US TO THINK ABOUT THE COFFEE WE DRINK IN A WAY WHICH DOESN'T MAKE OUR HEADS HURT'

As well as producing a pukka cup, the guys are also passionate about protecting the environment. From their depths-of-the-countryside Cornish HQ to the farms where the beans are grown, sustainability rules. A tree-planting initiative and a roastery powered by solar and biofuels are just the start of their carbon-offsetting commitments.

And the coffee? The Explore range leads enthusiasts on a journey through out-of-the-ordinary flavours and experimental profiles. And whichever variety you choose, the team strive to send beans packing from the roastery within 24 hours of roasting.

www.yallahcoffee.co.uk T: 01326 727383
f @yallahcoffee 🐦 @yallahcoffee 📷 @yallahcoffee

MORE GOOD

CUPS

So many exceptional places to drink coffee ...

№104
108 COFFEE HOUSE

108c Kenwyn Street, Truro,
Cornwall, TR1 3DJ

www.108coffee.co.uk

№105
ARTIGIANO

248 High Street, Exeter, Devon, EX4 3PZ

www.artigiano.uk.com

№106
BAYARDS COVE INN

27 Lower Street, Dartmouth,
Devon, TQ6 9AN

www.bayardscoveinn.co.uk

№107
BAYARDS KITCHEN

Shops at Dartington, Shinner's Bridge,
Totnes, Devon, TQ9 6TQ

www.bayardskitchen.co.uk

№108
BEACON COFFEE

28a High Street, Falmouth,
Cornwall, TR11 2AD

www.beaconcoffee.co.uk

№109
BIKE SHED CAFE

The Square, Barnstaple,
Devon, EX32 8LS

www.bikesheduk.com

№110
BLUE PIG CAFE

33 Colston Avenue, Bristol, BS1 4UA

www.bluepigcafe.co.uk

№111
BOO'S KITCHEN

Woodville Road, The Mumbles,
Swansea, SA3 4AD

112
BOSTON TEA PARTY – BARNSTAPLE
21-22 Tuly Street, Barnstaple, Devon, EX31 1DH
www.bostonteaparty.co.uk

113
BOSTON TEA PARTY – EXETER
84 Queen Street, Exeter, Devon, EX4 3RP
www.bostonteaparty.co.uk

114
BOSTON TEA PARTY – HONITON
Monkton House, 53 High Street, Honiton, Devon, EX14 1PW
www.bostonteaparty.co.uk

115
BOSTON TEA PARTY – PARK STREET
75 Park Street, Bristol, BS1 5PF
www.bostonteaparty.co.uk

116
BOX & BARBER
82 Fore Street, Newquay, Cornwall, TR7 1EY

117
BREW & BAKE
217 Bath Road, Cheltenham, Gloucestershire, GL53 7NA
www.brewandbake.coffee

118
BRODIES COFFEE CO
Gorsedd Gardens, Cardiff, CF10 3NP

119
CAFE AT 36
36 Cowick Street, Exeter, Devon, EX4 1AW

120
CHANDOS DELI – BATH
12 George Street, Bath, BA1 2EH
www.chandosdeli.com

121
CHANDOS DELI – EXETER
1 Roman Walk, Princesshay, Exeter, Devon, EX1 1GN
www.chandosdeli.com

122
CHARLIE FRIDAY'S COFFEE SHOP
Church Steps, Church Hill, Lynton, Devon, EX35 6HY
www.charliefridayscoffeeshop.co.uk

123
COASTERS COFFEE COMPANY
1 Abbots Quay, Prince of Wales Road, Kingsbridge, Devon, TQ7 1DY

124
COFFEE LAB UK
35 Blue Boar Row, Salisbury, Wiltshire, SP1 1DA
www.coffeelabuk.com

MAP 125
CREDITON COFFEE COMPANY

1 Market Square House, Market Street,
Crediton, Devon, EX17 2BN

www.creditoncoffee.co.uk

MAP 126
ESPRESSINI

39 Killigrew Street, Falmouth, Cornwall, TR11 3PW

MAP 127
ESPRESSINI DULCE

45 Arwenack Street, Falmouth, Cornwall, TR11 3JH

MAP 128
EXE COFFEE ROASTERS

19 Heavitree Road, Exeter, Devon, EX1 2LD

www.execoffeeroasters.co.uk

MAP 129
EXPLODING BAKERY

1b Central Station, Queen Street, Exeter,
Devon, EX4 3SB

www.explodingbakery.com

MAP 130
FIN & CO.

Above Watershed, 3-5 Bank Street,
Newquay, Cornwall, TR7 1EP

www.watershedbrand.com

MAP 131
FULL COURT PRESS

59 Broad Street, Bristol, BS1 2EJ

MAP 132
GINHAUS DELI

1 Market Street, Llandeilo,
Carmarthenshire, SA19 6AH

www.ginhaus.co.uk

MAP 133
GOOD VIBES CAFE

28 Killigrew Street, Falmouth,
Cornwall, TR11 3PN

MAP 134
GREENGAGES COFFEE HOUSE & RESTAURANT

31 Catherine Street, Salisbury,
Wiltshire, SP1 2DQ

www.greengagessalisbury.co.uk

MAP 135
HART'S BAKERY

Arch 35, Lower Approach Road, Temple
Meads, Bristol, BS1 6QS

www.hartsbakery.co.uk

MAP 136
HATTERS COFFEE HOUSE

21 Fore Street, Redruth, Cornwall, TR15 2BD

MAP 137
HUB ST IVES

4 The Wharf, St Ives, Cornwall, TR26 1LF

www.hub-stives.co.uk

138
HUBBOX BRISTOL
113 Whiteladies Road, Clifton, Bristol, BS8 2PB

www.hubbox.co.uk

139
JACKA BAKERY
38 Southside Street, Plymouth, Devon, PL1 2LE

140
KIN + ILK – CAPITAL QUARTER
1 Capital Quarter, Tyndall Street, Cardiff, CF10 4BZ

www.kinandilk.com

141
LEYKERS
1 White Hart Yard, Trowbridge, Wiltshire, BA14 8BY

www.leykers.co.uk

142
LIBERTY COFFEE
4 Northgate Street, Launceston, Cornwall, PL15 8BD

www.liberty-coffee.co.uk

143
THE LITTLE MAN COFFEE COMPANY – BRIDGE STREET
Ivor House, Bridge Street, Cardiff, CF10 2EE

www.littlemancoffee.co.uk

144
THE LITTLE MAN COFFEE COMPANY – TUDOR LANE
10 Tudor Lane, Cardiff, CF11 6AZ

www.littlemancoffee.co.uk

145
MILK TEETH
21 Portland Square, Bristol, BS2 8SJ

www.milkteethportlandsq.co.uk

146
MOCKINGBIRD
58 Alma Vale Road, Clifton, Bristol, BS8 2HS

147
MOKOKO COFFEE – ABBEY CHURCHYARD
6 Abbey Churchyard, Bath, BA1 1LY

www.mokokocoffee.com

148
NEW ENGLAND COFFEE HOUSE
1 Digbeth Street, Stow-on-the-Wold, Gloucestershire, GL54 1BN

www.newenglandcoffeehouse.com

149
NO12 EASTON
12 High Street, Easton, Bristol, BS5 6DL

150
OLIVE & CO.
Windsor Place, Liskeard, Cornwall, PL14 4BH

www.olivecocafe.com

151
ORIGIN COFFEE ROASTERS – HARBOUR HEAD
Harbour Head, Porthleven, Cornwall, TR13 9JY
www.origincoffee.co.uk

152
ORIGIN COFFEE ROASTERS – PENRYN
The Warehouse, Commerical Road,
Penryn, Cornwall, TR10 8AE
www.origincoffee.co.uk

153
PICNIC CORNWALL
14 Church Street, Falmouth, Cornwall, TR11 3DR
www.picniccornwall.co.uk

154
PINKMANS
85 Park Street, Bristol, BS1 5PJ
www.pinkmans.co.uk

155
RELISH FOOD & DRINK
Foundry Court, Wadebridge, Cornwall, PL27 7QN
www.relishcornwall.co.uk

156
RHUBARB & MUSTARD
11 Millbay Road, Plymouth, Devon, PL1 3LF

157
ROLLING ITALY
Woodland Road, Clifton, Bristol, BS8 1UH

158
SHOREDITCH WHITE
Corporation Street, Taunton,
Somerset, TA1 4AW
www.shoreditchwhite.com

159
SPICER+COLE – CLIFTON VILLAGE
9 Princess Victoria Street, Clifton Village,
Bristol, BS8 4DX
www.spicerandcole.co.uk

160
THE BREW HOUSE CAFE
8 High Street, Bideford, Devon, EX39 2AA

161
THE BRISTOLIAN CAFE
2 Picton Street, Montpelier, Bristol, BS6 5QA
www.thebristolian.co.uk

162
THE CHEEKY BEAN
12 Market Place, Shepton Mallet, BA4 5AZ
www.thecheekybean.co.uk

163
THE EARLY BIRD
38 Woodville Road, Cardiff, CF24 4EB
www.earlybirdbakery.co.uk

164
THE FORUM COFFEE HOUSE

1a Forum Buildings, St James's Parade, Bath, BA1 1UG

www.bathforum.co.uk

165
THE GREEN BIRD CAFE

11 Margaret's Buildings, Bath, BA1 2LP

www.greenbirdcafe.co.uk

166
THE GREEN ROCKET

1 Pierrepont Street, Bath, BA1 1LB

www.thegreenrocket.co.uk

167
THE HAIRY BARISTA

69 High Street, Totnes, Devon, TQ9 5PB

168
THE STORES

1 St Mary's Road, Croyde, EX33 1LF

www.thestorescroyde.co.uk

169
UPRISING

59 Magdalen Road, Exeter, EX2 4TA

www.uprising.space

170
WATERLOO TEA – LAKESIDE

17-19 Clearwater Way, Lakeside, Cardiff, CF23 6DL

www.waterlootea.com

171
WATERLOO TEA – PENARTH

1-3 Washington Buildings, Stanwell Road, Penarth, CF64 2AD

www.waterlootea.com

172
WATERLOO TEA – PENYLAN

5 Waterloo Gardens, Penylan, Cardiff, CF23 5AA

www.waterlootea.com

173
WATERLOO TEA – WYNDHAM ARCADE

21-25 Wyndham Arcade, The Hayes, Cardiff, CF10 1FH

www.waterlootea.com

174
WEST STREET KITCHEN

55 West Street, Bristol, BS2 0BZ

www.weststreetkitchen.co.uk

175
WILD VIBES CAFE

Argal and College Water Park, Mabe Burnthouse, Penryn, Cornwall, TR10 9JF

176
WRIGHTS FOOD EMPORIUM

Golden Grove Arms, Llanarthne, Carmarthenshire, SA32 8JU

www.wrightsfood.co.uk

MORE GOOD ROASTERS

Additional hot hauls for your hopper

MAP Nº 177
BUNABERRY COFFEE ROASTERS

Unit 5 Station Road Workshops, Station Road, Bristol, BS15 4PJ
www.bunaberry.com

MAP Nº 178
CLIFTON COFFEE ROASTERS

Unit C2, Island Trade Park, Bristow Broadway, Avonmouth, Bristol, BS11 9FB
www.cliftoncoffee.co.uk

MAP Nº 179
COLONNA COFFEE

Unit 5, Apollo Park, Armstrong Way, Yate, Bristol, BS37 5AH
www.colonnacoffee.com

MAP Nº 180
CREDITON COFFEE COMPANY

1 Market Square House, Market Street, Crediton, Devon, EX17 2BN
www.creditoncoffee.co.uk

MAP Nº 181
EXE COFFEE ROASTERS

19 Heavitree Road, Exeter, Devon, EX1 2LD
www.execoffeeroasters.co.uk

MAP Nº 182
FINCA COFFEE ROASTERS

Unit 101, 20-22 The Grove, Dorchester, Dorset, DT1 1ST
www.fincacoffee.co.uk

MAP Nº 183
FOOTPRINT COFFEE

Ednol Farm, Kinnerton, Presteigne, Powys, LD8 2PF
www.footprintcoffee.co.uk

MAP Nº 184
JAMES GOURMET COFFEE CO

Chase Industrial Estate, Alton Road, Ross-on-Wye, Herefordshire, HR9 5WA
www.jamesgourmetcoffee.com

MAP № 185
LITTLESTONE COFFEE
17 Norman Court, Budlake Road, Exeter, Devon, EX2 8PY

www.littlestonecoffee.co.uk

MAP № 186
LUFKIN COFFEE ROASTERS
183a Kings Road, Cardiff, CF11 9DF

www.lufkincoffee.com

MAP № 187
MANUMIT
Cardiff

www.manumitcoffee.co.uk

MAP № 188
OLFACTORY COFFEE ROASTERS
The Old Brewery Yard, Lower Treluswell, Penryn, Cornwall, TR10 9AT

www.olfactorycoffee.co.uk

MAP № 189
ORIGIN COFFEE ROASTERS
The Roastery, Wheal Vrose Business Park, Helston, Cornwall, TR13 0FG

www.origincoffee.co.uk

MAP № 190
QUANTUM COFFEE ROASTERS
58 Bute Street, Quayside, Cardiff, CF10 5BN

www.quantumcoffeeroasters.co.uk

MAP № 191
RAVE COFFEE
Unit 7, Stirling Works, Love Lane, Cirencester, Gloucestershire, GL7 1YG

www.ravecoffee.co.uk

MAP № 192
READS COFFEE
Limekiln Farm, Thornford Road, Sherborne, Dorset, DT9 6PS

www.readscoffee.co.uk

MAP № 193
RISING GROUND
Unit 9, Foundry Court, Wadebridge, Cornwall, PL27 7QN

www.risingground.coffee

MAP № 194
ROUND HILL ROASTERY
Unit 14, Midsomer Enterprise Park, Midsomer Norton, Somerset, BA3 2BB

www.roundhillroastery.com

MAP № 195
TRIPLE CO ROAST
11 Charles Street, Stokes Croft, Bristol, BS1 3NN

www.triplecoroast.com

MAP № 196
VOYAGER COFFEE
Unit 6, Mardle Way, Business Park, Buckfastleigh, Devon, TQ11 0JL

www.voyagercoffee.co.uk

MEET OUR COMMITTEE

Our *Independent Coffee Guide* committee is made up of a small band of leading coffee experts from across the region who have worked with Salt Media and the South West and South Wales' speciality community to oversee the creation of this book

RICHARD BLAKE

Roasting with the original crew at Extract in the early days, Rich learnt most of what he knows about green coffee, trading, roasting and brewing at the Bristol roastery before leaving to launch his own business, Yallah Coffee, in 2014. As a keen surfer and outdoor adventurer, the Cornish countryside was the natural choice in which to house his lovingly restored 1950s roaster. Sustainability, involvement in social enterprises and supporting communities reliant on the coffee chain are all high on the Yallah agenda.

CALLUM PARSONS

Starting his coffee career at Extract Coffee in 2014, Callum is now the South West and Midlands regional manager for the Bristol roastery and stocks coffee shops in his patch with lip-smackingly good beans.

When he's not competing in national comps and touring the country crafting coffee, the two-time UK Barista Championship finalist indulges his second passion: wine. Callum says: *'I often bring wine into a new conversation about speciality coffee as it's something many people can relate to in terms of how much it's affected by climate, origin and varietal.'*

DAVE STANTON

After catching the coffee bug down under, Dave returned to the UK eager to master the art of roasting. Fuelling his passion by professionally pouring brews by day, he spent his nights (for several years) experimenting on his home roaster. Dave finally took the leap into professional roasting in 2014, launching Crankhouse Coffee from his garage in Exeter. Moving his operation to new premises in 2017 gave him more space in which to play. Crankhouse now stocks speciality coffee houses across the country with its collection of high quality blends and single origin beans.

COFFEE NOTES

Somewhere to save details of specific brews and
beans you've enjoyed

INDEX

INDEX